Women, Violence and Tradition

About the Editor

Tamsin Bradley is Lecturer in International Development at the University of Portsmouth, and was previously Principal Lecturer in Anthropology and Director of the International Centre for Community Development in the Faculty of Applied Social Science at London Metropolitan University. Her research focuses on Indian religions and culture and examines the impact of gender and international development work on the lives of local people. She is co-director of the Dowry Project which combines theory and practice in the pursuit of human rights for women. Her key publications include *Religion and Gender in the Developing World* (2010) and, with Emma Tomalin and Mangala Subramaniam, *Dowry: Bridging the Gap between Theory and Practice* (2009).

Women, Violence and Tradition

Taking FGM and other
practices to a secular state

Edited by
TAMSIN BRADLEY

Zed Books
LONDON & NEW YORK

Women, Violence and Tradition: Taking FGM and other practices to a secular state was first published in 2011 by Zed Books Ltd, 7 Cynthia Street, London N1 9JF, UK, and Room 400, 175 Fifth Avenue, New York, NY 10010, USA

www.zedbooks.co.uk

Typeset in Great Britain by Free Range Book Design & Production Limited
Index: Rohan Bolton, rohan.indexing@gmail.com
Cover designed by Alice Marwick, www.alice-marwick.co.uk
Printed and bound in Great Britain by MPG Books, Bodmin and King's Lynn

Mixed Sources
Product group from well-managed forests and other controlled sources
www.fsc.org Cert no. SA-COC-1565
© 1996 Forest Stewardship Council
FSC

Distributed in the USA exclusively by Palgrave Macmillan, a division of St Martin's Press, LLC, 175 Fifth Avenue, New York, NY 10010, USA

A catalogue record for this book is available from the British Library
Library of Congress Cataloging in Publication Data available

ISBN 978 1 84813 959 6 hb
ISBN 978 1 84813 958 9 pb

Contents

Acknowledgements

There are many people to thank for this volume. I have to begin by thanking my wonderful anthropology and community development students at London Metropolitan University. Although some of them are in their own right authors of this volume, they have received support and encouragement from their peers. We have enjoyed together many heated debates out of which we came to realise how important a volume such as this really is. I would also like to acknowledge colleagues who have supported this venture: the Dean of the Faculty of Social Sciences, Professor John Gabriel; Academic Leader in Social Sciences, Peter Hodgkinson; and Associate Dean Brian Hall. On a daily basis both the authors and I have received support and encouragement from Lynda Reaich, Anne Massey, Zafar Khan, Sami Ramadani, Brian Mcdonough, Jenny Harding and Tara Young. I know the students/authors behind this volume would not have developed as writers and critical thinkers without the excellent teaching and commitment of many inspiring lecturers, including those listed above.

This volume is dedicated to the women whose stories are recounted in it and they deserve the greatest acknowledgement for their courage and willingness to participate, to become part of it. This volume is intended to make a positive contribution, however small, to their lives.

We must also acknowledge the work of dedicated activists and practitioners who respond on a daily basis to the abuse suffered by black and minority ethnic (BME) women. Hannana Siddiqui is one such activist who along with her colleagues at Southall Black Sisters (SBS) works tirelessly to push for change and to support women who come forward to change their lives for the better. This volume is also for SBS in the hope that it might support their campaigns and help evidence their political visions. Any profits awarded to the authors will be donated to Southall Black Sisters. It seems only right that this volume contributes in every way possible towards a better and more equal society for all.

About the Contributors

Isha Abulkadir is in her final year of a BA in Anthropology and Sociology, Faculty of Applied Social Sciences, London Metropolitan University. She is an activist working specifically with the Somali communities in London to end the practice of female genital mutilation.

Ebyan Ahmed has successfully completed her BA in Anthropology and Sociology, Faculty of Applied Social Sciences, London Metropolitan University. She is now pursuing her career as a paramedic and works to promote cultural awareness in the health service.

Esline Dzumbunu is in her final year of a BA in Anthropology and Sociology. She enrolled on her degree following a career as a banker. She also works as a volunteer for the Salvation Army and advocates on behalf of the homeless.

Noorjahan Begum has completed a BSc in Community Sector Management, Faculty of Applied Social Sciences, London Metropolitan University. She now works for a research-focused community organisation in Tower Hamlets where she promotes the rights of ethnic minority women.

Charlenie Naik has completed her BSc in Psychology and Social Anthropology, Faculty of Applied Social Sciences, London Metropolitan University. She is now pursuing postgraduate studies in anthropology and hopes to work in international development.

Sana Khilji is completing her BA in Anthropology and Sociology, Faculty of Applied Social Sciences, London Metropolitan University, following which she intends to work for a community organisation in London.

Hannana Siddiqui is head of policy and research for Southall Black Sisters and co-founder of Women Against Fundamentalism. She has published widely on the rights of BME women, including (with P. Patel), 'Shrinking Secular Spaces: Asian Women at the Intersect of Race, Religion and Gender' in R. Thiara and A. Gill (eds), *Violence against Women in South Asian Communities: Issues for Policy and Practice* (2010).

Introduction

This volume began in a seminar room three years ago with a discussion into the ethics of anthropological research and the responsibilities of fieldworkers towards the people they study. A hand went up and one of my Somali students began to tell us why studying anthropology is so important to her. I will never forget the conversation in which she told the class, 'I am here because I want to challenge practices within my own culture, specifically "female genital mutilation" [FGM]. It happened to me and has ruined parts of my life; I do not want it to happen to my sisters or children.' I looked around the class and saw some of my students in tears; I realised then my responsibility to manage their shock at this close encounter with an experience far removed from their Western secular lives, but mostly to Isha for whom this conversation marked a significant step in her personal quest to change attitudes towards women's bodies in Somali culture. This volume is an important opportunity for Isha and other similarly minded black minority ethnic (BME) women to explore, record and give voice to women's experiences, positive and negative, of their cultural and religious heritage. It represents an important platform and space upon and within which challenges towards aspects of tradition are articulated whilst other dimensions are acknowledged for the security and sense of identity, purpose and empowerment they provide.

The importance of this volume for the women who have researched and written it is summarised by their own comments:

> This book is an opportunity for me to try and change things in my culture so that other girls don't have to suffer the way I did.

I want this book to set the record straight. I don't want people to think my culture oppresses women or that Muslim women are weak. I love my heritage and it is important to me that this book should be a celebration but also highlight the things that do need to be challenged.

Researching my chapter gave me the chance to fill in bits of my own life history that I did not know about. I have cried a lot but also found great courage and strength in the stories women have shared with me. It has made me think about the contribution I want to make to the women of my community; this book is just the start.

This volume documents the contemporary life histories of women from diaspora communities in the UK, focusing specifically on their experiences of selected gendered practices and/or gender violence. Cultural and religious practices exist in every context, including secular states such as the UK. This volume explores how specific traditions such as female circumcision, dowry, marriage and divorce may or may not be reshaped or even eradicated under the influences of secularism. The volume is intended to explore what happens when secular values are brought into a relationship with the different beliefs underpinning religious and cultural traditions. What impact does this potential clash of worldviews, secular and religious, have on the lives of diaspora women? Has it resulted in at least some women rejecting aspects of their religious and cultural heritage in favour of a more secular and perhaps liberal approach to life? Or maybe women have found their religious and cultural identities even more important because they enable them to find a comfortable place within this diverse and often hostile state. In short, this book gives close insight into how black minority ethnic women today navigate between their religious and cultural traditions and the secular state. It tackles the sensitive and controversial issue of female genital mutilation, and surveys changing attitudes and practices around marriage and divorce. The cross-cultural perspective of this work draws in the views of activists and community organisations, specifically in Chapter 8, who work with women to confront injustice. Violence is a common thread throughout this volume, emerging out of the stories of many of the women included, and its eradication a constant concern for community organisations such as Southall Black Sisters (SBS) to whom the editor's income from the book will be given.

The contention surrounding the labelling of specific practices such as female genital mutilation (FGM) as 'cultural' and/or religious will be covered shortly. To avoid essentialist and reductionalist explanations into the foundations of the experiences covered in this volume, the terms 'gender practices' or 'gender violence' will be used to denote the complex prism of interlocking factors at the heart of each narrative recorded here. Within this prism, culture and religion represent just two of the strands. The book intends to give close insight into how black minority ethnic women navigate between their religious and cultural traditions and the secular state in the UK. The stories in this volume also reveal how the marginalisation experienced by some women because of divorce, forced marriage, dowry or FGM are intensified and even sanctioned by the ignorance of the secular legislative system and so-called state support services, which are often unwilling to intervene in matters deemed to be 'cultural'. The book will illuminate areas of tension and difficulty when some women actively try and reform aspects of their tradition whilst remaining passionately loyal to their cultural and religious identities. Other examples will highlight how young women are choosing to endorse traditional practices, seeing this as an important way of demonstrating the legitimacy of their religion and culture in the face of increasing hostility from the wider communities in which they live. Both sets of responses reveal a lack of state support and examples given here reveal the limited exit options provided by wider society and state apparatuses in the UK. Although the research here focuses on the experiences of diaspora women in the UK, it is likely that many of the stories will resonate with women across the globe.

The practices and themes of this volume have emerged during initial fieldwork but also represent topics that are underresearched in current literature. The intention is to delve into areas that have previously been approached at a distance primarily through medical, legal or human rights texts. Research often fails to explore holistically the complexities of an issue, which can only be done by unravelling the multiple layers of black minority ethnic (BME) women's experiences of living in the UK.

This book's main argument asserts that BME women view their cultural heritage as one of the important lenses through which they negotiate everyday life and make sense of the world they live in. This volume will also argue that different women of the same cultural group and generation frequently hold opposing views on what is positive about their heritage. This volume will argue overall that the intersections between religion, culture, race, ethnicity and patriarchy still maintain gender relations that leave many women vulnerable to social, economic and political marginalisation as well as to different forms of violence. Violence is highlighted throughout this work as a cross-cultural problem which is inherently gendered. Violence against women emerges either as a result of specific practices such as female genital mutilation or in domestic settings as a mechanism used by men (and in a small number of cases also women) to ensure women behave 'appropriately' according to the so-called norms of their patriarchal culture. Feminist literature has for some time argued that female bodies across the globe are used by dominant forces in each society as symbols of collective honour. Greater focus is therefore placed on ensuring female bodies conform and uphold the values and beliefs of that community. The stories here highlight again the scrutiny women come under both within their diaspora community and also in wider society. The stories also reveal the extent to which the secular state, through its lack of engagement with the specific experiences of BME women, supports gender violence.

The initial intention was not to write a book about violence against women, but rather to document how diaspora women uphold, challenge and defend aspects of their tradition within the dominant secular state; however, as the research got under way this objective changed. It became clear that no matter what the starting point was in the retelling of the life stories, many of the women reported experiences of different forms of violence, abuse and oppression. In presenting these narratives the contributors have significant responsibility to do so sensitively and accurately, and ensure they do not represent experiences of violence simplistically. The violence documented in this volume is fundamentally the result of a gender ideology that devalues women and supports the right of men to dominate. The authors therefore were wary of presenting violence as a 'cultural problem'. Rather, the ways in which different women talk about and confront forms of violence in their lives is the focus, which results in nuanced and holistic pictures of women's lives emerging.

The primary contribution this work makes is seen in the first-hand and detailed accounts of diaspora women's lives. There is very little cross-cultural contemporary data that seeks to record directly the voices and experiences of BME women. The topics covered are highly sensitive and delicate and required careful ethical consideration in terms of how they were approached, recorded and then represented through this text. The research team behind this volume includes anthropology and community development undergraduate students from the Faculty of Applied Social Sciences, London Metropolitan University, who are themselves black minority ethnic women. They have collected the life stories of other women from within their communities. The researchers have been mentored by the editor who has also ensured that the project complies with ethical research standards as set by the university and also professional bodies such as the Royal Anthropological Institute and Association of Social Anthropology.

The material contained here represents new stories and perspectives on the quickly changing world we live in, but, and perhaps more significantly, these are the stories the women featured wanted to be told. The research reflects and documents the different views and experiences women have had living through this ever more global and insecure era. The material will look to highlight the impact that world events such as 9/11 have had on the way in which women perceive their own cultures and the forms of expression they draw on to identify themselves to others inside and outside of their immediate community. In other words, have certain practices increased as a result of women feeling that their cultural heritage is being negatively stereotyped, judged and marginalised? Is female circumcision on the increase among certain groups of women? If yes, how then do feminist organisations respond to the determination of some women to preserve practices that are seen by many inside and outside these cultures as brutal and unjust?

The lack of contemporary data documenting the different experiences of black minority ethnic women is surprising given that responding to marginalised groups continues to be a key area of government policy and concern, plus a topic of media and public interest. Archives such as those held by the Women's Library at London Metropolitan University are frequently approached by community groups and policy makers who request current data to help inform their projects and programmes. This book is intended to provide material that potentially could inform the work of community organisations, other non-governmental organisations and policy makers. The current global concerns over terrorism and security have led to even more cultural stereotyping and increases in racial prejudice and assumptions. There is a lack of material that considers the impact these changed times are having on how black minority ethnic women identify themselves and how they visualise their futures and place in the world. The perceptions of BME women must be documented in order to understand how and where new forms of feminist activism exist and where national policy and campaigns should be positioned.

Women, Violence and Tradition is not exclusively about culture and tradition but focuses on women's narratives and reflections about their lives in the UK. In some chapters the stories told are transnational in that some women recount their experiences of practices such as dowry and FGM which took place in their country of birth, prior to their migration to the UK. In their narratives they are reflecting and recreating for this volume their memories of these practices and offering an interpretation of them that is shaped not just by their cultural and religious heritage but also the secular values of the state which is now their home. It is likely that their views and indeed memories of their experiences of these practices have shifted over time as a result of being exposed, through migration, to a diverse range of responses to their heritage. It is possible that a practice for many years they happily complied with and upheld they now view differently and reject. It may also be that some women always felt, for example, that

FGM was wrong, but living in a secular state has provided a different framework of concepts and language through which to articulate resistance and challenge oppression.

Some definitions

Despite the broad emphasis on life histories, bound up in the stories in many chapters are descriptions of specific practices, such as female circumcision, Islamic marriage and divorce practices and the Hindu practice of *dowry*. It is therefore important that some of the practices covered are defined. *Female circumcision* refers to a practice now more commonly referred to in literature as *genital female cutting*. Although there are various forms of the practice it involves the removal of all of or part of a young girl's clitoris. As detailed in Chapter 3, the term circumcision is used because it translates directly into African languages and because researchers have found that using the label *female genital mutilation* (FGM) alienates those who still support the practice. For this reason a third term has emerged, *genital cutting*, which is hoped to be less politicised, offering a literal description of what happens in this practice. However, FGM is the term largely used in this volume, chosen by the author of Chapter 2 because of her own experiences of this practice. FGM is illegal in the UK, with the most recent legislative change put in place in 2003. Chapters 3 and 5 present women's stories of Islamic marriage and divorce in the Bangladeshi and Somali communities in the UK. Significant diversity exists between Muslim cultures but essentially *Islamic marriage* takes place during a ceremony called the *nikkah* which is the contract drawn up and signed between the bride and groom. Chapter 6 compares the life histories of upper caste *Brahmin* Hindu women in the UK. The chapter focuses on the practice of *dowry* which is defined as a financial transaction between the bride's family and her new in-laws at the point of marriage, in which money and/or goods are given by the bride's family in exchange for her marriage. No real research has been conducted on dowry in the UK but work carried out into the practice in India suggests that dowry is a significant factor in many instances of violence against women (Bradley and Tomalin, 2009). Dowry is illegal in India but legislation in the UK against dowry is not in place, leaving women vulnerable to the same atrocities and harassments after marriage (http://news.bbc.co.uk/1/hi/uk/8093948.stm). Although the research presented here does not reveal stories of dowry abuse, it does make visible the extent to which the practice is still observed by Hindus in the UK. The stories also highlight the extent to which dowry is founded upon a patriarchal gender ideology that considers women inferior to men; these beliefs are in themselves highly problematic for women. Forms of *domestic violence* emerge in the life stories given in chapters 4 and 5. Domestic violence in this volume is understood to refer literally to violence within the home and can include psychological as well as physical abuse.

Ethical risks and the essentialist trap

The compiling of this research was not without ethical risks and exposes all involved – but specifically the editor – to a variety of post-colonial and orientalist critiques. For example, I run the risk of replicating the misguided research that scholars such as Narayan so convincingly critique. Narayan's now famous work (1997) accuses some Western feminist academics of reducing the violence and oppression suffered by non-Western women to matters of culture, religion and tradition. She coined the phrase 'death by culture' and claimed that the same cultural explanations are not given to the often similar abuses that white, Western women suffer from:

> I intend to argue that when such 'cultural explanations' are given for *fatal* forms of violence against Third World women, the effect is to suggest that Third World women suffer 'death by culture'. I shall try and show that fatal forms of violence against mainstream Western women seem interestingly resistant to such 'cultural explanations', leaving Western women seemingly more immune to 'death by culture'. I believe that such asymmetries in 'cultural explanation' result in pictures of Third World women as 'victims of their culture' in ways that are interestingly different from the way in which victimisation of mainstream Western women is understood. (1997: 84–85; emphasis in original)

Kelly echoes elements of Narayan's critique in the preface to an important edited collection, *Violence against South Asian Women* (Thiara and Gill, 2010): 'This volume also challenges simplistic notions of culture, whether drawn on to explain or "otherwise" certain forms of VAW or to position BME women and the organisations that support them outside of the mainstream. At the same time, issues of culture form a backdrop to the experiences of minority women and how they are responded to' (2010: 12).

This book is founded upon a 'life histories' approach that seeks to sensitively draw out women's own responses and experiences, focusing on the stories they want to tell. As already stated, some of these stories focus specifically on domestic violence, others link violence to specific cultural practices such as FGM, some talk about forms of oppression linked in part to experiences of marriage and divorce. Each story, although retold in isolation, has to be analysed against the wider secular and multicultural society in which these women live. I am careful not to make direct links between culture, tradition and violence, ever mindful of the warnings of the dangers of culturalising violence against women (see also Erturk, 2007).

Cultures are not fixed and unchanging and this book attempts through the stories recorded to highlight how shifts in attitudes are brought about because of the varied way in which women and men experience and respond to their lives and are constantly renegotiating aspects of their identity. Theoretically in this Introduction I set out how *intersectionality* enables a more sophisticated and nuanced analysis to emerge that helps researchers to avoid essentialising and stereotyping the experiences of BME women on the grounds of their cultural identity. The approach taken in collecting the stories is useful not only because it allows others to speak and so destabilises the authority of the author and researcher, but also because it allows the complexities of context to emerge. As the stories documented here reveal, a simple account of marriage can quickly lead to testimonies of psychological and/or physical abuse. The researchers involved have shown their bravery in listening to and respectfully recording these stories. The stories have been painstakingly collected often over several meetings and reveal a shocking pattern of normalisation in which misogynistic patriarchal gender ideologies cross-culturally shape women's lives, resulting in some cases in various forms of violent injustices but almost always in some form of exclusion or marginalisation. The research also reveals how the storytellers acknowledge the importance of their cultural and religious identity in making sense of the injustices they face and draw on their heritage to navigate a more positive sense of self. Nothing is new in the argument that women across the world have to exist in and resist the oppressive forces of patriarchy, but this book allows individual women to reflect on personal battles and experiences and collectively enables the researchers to draw some conclusions about the impact migration has had or not had in reasserting or eradicating particular practices.

Focused research on the differing experiences BME women have of migration is limited. Most work has been done on the experiences of south Asian women. For example, Thiara and Gill, editors of *Violence against Women in South Asian Communities: Issues for policy and practice* (2005), state that knowledge about the lives of diaspora south Asian women is fragmented and the purpose of their volume is to bring together a body of writing by activists and researchers engaged in contemporary debates about gender, race, racism, ethnicity, culture and violence. For Thiara and Gill and their contributors, violence against south Asian women must be understood as mediated through the intersections of systems of domination based on race, ethnicity, class, culture and nationality. Therefore emphasis should be placed on how structures of power are created and lead to the marginalisation of groups rather than simply focusing on cultural differences. It is only through such a critical approach that a detailed comprehension of south Asian women's personal and collective experience, both theoretically and practically, will be gained. Sokoloff and Dupont (2005) argue the need to emphasise the structural underpinnings of abuse while not denying the existence of real difference among women. For Thiara and Gill, 'culture' and 'faith' are important in the lives of south Asian women. However, they state that 'the contributions in this book all allude to the importance of considering culture as a dynamic and contested force rather than as a static and unchanging monolith. It is thus both a source of oppression and support for women' (2010:

33). This view is echoed in the stories given in this book and as I describe later, women draw on and use the categories of religion and culture to explain abuse but also to help them navigate and challenge it. Bhachu (1993) notes how diaspora south Asian women constantly reinvent and reproduce cultural values and norms. She uses the term 'cultural entrepreneurs' to describe the fluid way in which culture and religion are used by women as they resist abuse but constantly reconstruct positive self-images against a backdrop of racism and social marginalisation. A contradiction emerges in that women also enact versions of culture that perpetuate the interests of the patriarchal community even if it is not in their interests. Some of the accounts in this volume (chapters 2, 3, 6) also seem to suggest that women do knowingly collude with the very structures that have oppressed them. On first reading the stories in these chapters this compliance with, and submission to, patriarchy could be easily misinterpreted as weakness. However, as the stories in chapters 2 and 6 show, even compliance with patriarchy is carefully calculated and usually only opted for when a women feels there are no other choices. In other words, women may stay in an abusive status quo because the wider state structures have not provided support and understanding: there are simply no exit options available. To be blunt, numerous stories told in these pages highlight how the secular state condemns many BME women to a life of painful compliance even though if alternatives existed they would choose otherwise.

This book suggests that migration to the UK has done little to really challenge the particular forms of oppression BME women face, in that the practices and abusive behaviours documented still go on. In fact there is evidence, as Siddiqui suggests in her chapter, that diaspora women are becoming more marginalised by the secular state's engagement with 'faith communities' led by men. Engagement with so-called faith communities now represents a key strategy in the war against terror. Underlying this policy is the assumption that male leaders understand and can represent the experience of all members of their communities. Chapters 2 and 4 clearly show that religious leaders are complicit in supporting gender violence and do not adequately acknowledge or respond to the injustices women suffer.

The stories in this volume also reveal a growing confidence and increase in self-belief among women who often do want change, but on their terms. This book also gives voice to the activism of the researchers behind the chapters, some of whom in Chapter 1 talk honestly about the importance of raising the visibility of different groups of BME women and their specific experiences of injustice. The very fact that these researchers, some with their own stories of abuse to tell, have taken their place at university gives ground for optimism. The state has opened the door of higher education just enough to allow some BME women from poorer families the chance to strengthen their voice and take their experiences to a wider audience. However, this door may soon shut again as a shift in the political landscape drags us back into social exclusion under the guise of so-called 'fairness', which should denote a sense of justice but in reality seems to be used to justify the withdrawal of resources from minority and marginal groups in the name of efficiency. This shift from 'equality' to 'fairness' is concerning as it fails to draw critical attention to the ways in which BME women battle injustices. 'Fairness' also fails to project a clear vision of the type of world we should be aiming to create. 'Equality' on the other hand shapes an ideal vision of society in which women from all groups can live without fear and with the state's support. Unless government officials and civil servants continue to strive to understand how inequalities are produced and impact on different peoples' lives, especially those of BME women, many individuals will find themselves slipping even more deeply into marginal spaces.

Diaspora women should be supported in staking out further a platform from which to share their stories, otherwise government policy will remain dependent on negative and distorting stereotypes about the lives of 'other' BME women. For example, significant resources have been poured into government research into honour killings and forced marriage, whilst much less is known about other related practices such as dowry, which according to community activists such as Southall Black Sisters is at the heart of many of the cases they deal with. In short, we are only just beginning to produce more visible and sophisticated insights into the complex lives of BME women both positive and problematic. Much more work is needed, not least because little is known about the distinct and similar experiences of women within diaspora groups across the globe. For example, as Chapter 4 attests, little or no work has been conducted on Zimbabwean diaspora women's experiences of domestic violence in the UK. Nor do we know much about the prevalence of dowry among *Brahmins* in Manchester (Chapter 7). The dangers of not knowing are that outsiders make assumptions that feed into unhelpful and destructive stereotypes about the lives of 'other' women that are positioned in opposition to the secular category of liberated white, middle-class women (see Mohanty's (1995) argument summarised below).

Similar arguments are made by Wilson (2006), whose accounts of south Asian women's experiences of migrating to the UK expose systematic abuse and discrimination both within their family but also by the state. Wilson describes how state-level explanations attribute south Asian women's problems to their 'isolation' from the rest of UK society. She argues that the word 'isolation' is loaded with assumed implications. It suggests that women are passive victims of circumstances which are beyond anyone's control. It serves to mask patriarchal violence and racist exclusion and the reality of women's struggle against them (2005: 115). She vividly demonstrates this through numerous case studies that show the extent to which state agents and structures ignore or dismiss south Asian women's experiences of distress, isolation and violence. In one case she recounts how a woman whose husband beat her suffered post-natal depression and was then diagnosed with schizophrenia. Her daughter asked the consultant psychiatrist who had been in charge of her mother's case if he knew about the violence she had faced from her husband, and if he did, why he had chosen to ignore it. His answer was: 'I knew your father was dominant but we did not want the marriage to break down.' As Wilson states, 'patriarchal violence thus showed up as a matter of policy' (2006: 117). This example also shows how mental illness is exacerbated or even triggered as a result of patriarchal control, because vulnerable excluded women are pushed even further into isolation, predominantly by husbands.

Women without English and/or knowledge of how the system works find themselves unable to ask for help when they struggle to cope with the demands of being a wife and mother. As Wilson highlights, this is particularly acute during pregnancy, childbirth and young motherhood, when women need the support of medical professionals but find it hard to access them. The state fails to make itself accessible to these groups at these crucial times and so becomes complicit in the same oppressive behaviour exercised by husbands. Husbands manipulate situations and use mental diagnosis in order to win custody or to get rid of unwanted wives. As Wilson states:

> Asian women's experiences show that often their distress is a response to the violence they face. The government has declared that it is committed to eliminating violence but the way its agencies operate, particularly those involved with mental health, does not reflect this commitment. On the contrary, they collude with south Asian patriarchal violence. Too often the treatment given to women diagnosed as mentally disturbed is deeply disempowering and the racism and patriarchal relations which are part and parcel of life in mental institutions add a new dimension to their suffering. (2005: 127)

Wilson also echoes much of Patel's and Siddiqui's (2010) argument that the shift from multiculturalism to community cohesion and the prioritising of dialogues with male and faith and community leaders is already having a detrimental effect, increasing the levels of patriarchal control south Asian women face. This pattern will very likely also bear through in the experiences of other BME women although there is much less written on other groups. The recent funding squeeze has also destabilised the capacity local women's organisations have to respond to this increase in oppressive control and violence. This volume is very much intended to add yet more evidence to this argument that resources now have to be diverted into supporting specialised community groups who are best placed to respond to the changing and emerging needs of different groups of BME women.

Gender, religion and culture as part of an intersectional approach

The volume edited by Puwar and Raghuram (2003) builds upon the now well underway critique of the racial and gender prejudices of dominant discourses. They argue that little space exists 'for constructing or expressing alternative narratives that allow for the complexity of south Asian women's subjectivities or localities without the entrapments of completeness or closure' (2003: 12). Their book was intended to 'unsettle contemporary academic accounts, to shift the terms of the debate and to initiate new dialogues' (2003: 12). The particular contribution made by Ahmed (2002) stresses the urgent need to understand and critique the saliency of religion as a trope in both Western and south Asian geopolitics. She states that 'the complex ways gender interpolates with religion in the construction of heroic tales of Western imperialism must be interrogated' (2002: 13). These tales have been reaffirmed in the aftermath of 9/11 with even greater scrutiny from government, organisations and individuals being placed on the behaviour of south Asian and particularly Muslim women, whose bodies have become symbolic of their cultural and religious traditions. Islam has been repackaged and presented through dominant imperialist discourses as 'the problem' and once again the lives and supposed oppression of Muslim women presented as the evidence of a problematic tradition (Abu-Ludhod, 2002). The secular French state latched onto a constructed image of the oppressed veiled Muslim woman, projecting it as evidence of the threat Islam poses to a distinctly French concept of freedom and liberty (Wing and Smith, 2008). The stories in chapters 3 and 5 should also be placed against the backdrop of this resurgence in condemnation of Islam. The researchers themselves are from the traditions they write about and talk openly in Chapter 1 about the changing ways they have had to navigate their religious and cultural identities against the post-9/11 secular fears about the perceived evils of their traditions.

Some argue that too much emphasis is placed on culture and religion in seeking explanations as to why certain harmful practices exist. The secular feminist argument made by scholars such as Kelly

(2005) is direct in stating that patriarchal oppression is universal and although it weaves its way into the fabric of societies differently it is this ultimate dominance of a certain masculinity that is responsible for the injustices women suffer. Whilst this study endorses this view, the process through which patriarchy weaves itself into different cultures and communities is of interest to us here. Culture and religion are two dimensions of an analytical web that should be employed in a similar way to unpick all forms of oppression. Mohanty (1995) has famously argued that outsiders – specifically those engaged in Western feminist discourse – have a tendency to exoticise the lives of Third World women, condemning them as victims of brutal traditions from which they need freeing. Additionally, this narrow value-laden perspective fails to understand the complexities of why cultural practices may be simultaneously challenged and endorsed by women (see Bradley, 2006, 2009 and 2010). The process of supporting women's empowerment is not as simple as identifying practices that are harmful and suggesting they be eradicated. Through greater and more sensitive communication and dialogue, both with and between different groups of BME women, we can build appreciation of the various ways in which they individually and collectively challenge patriarchy and the unsupportive secular state in the UK.

Culture specifically remains an important part of the analytical web helping to unpack 'why' injustices happen, not least because, in the life histories presented in this volume, it consistently forms at least part of the explanation women present for the problems they face. Culture and religion have to be placed alongside gender, race and class as the key factors that form this analytical web which in turn shapes a person's positioning, identity and experiences. Crenshaw (1989) coined the term 'intersectionality' to describe the various social factors that produce the social inequalities women experience. Intersectionality focuses on the interrelationships of gender, class, race and ethnicity which come together in varying ways, shaping differing forms of discrimination women find themselves subject to. Yuval-Davis (2010) states that 'intersectionality has been at the core of the work of Asian feminists for decades' (2010: 9). The term is a popular analytical concept used by bodies such as the UN and many NGOs (non-governmental organisations). Yuval-Davis (2006) quotes from the fifty-eighth session of the UN Commission on Human Rights which in its first paragraph 'recognized the importance of examining the intersection of multiple forms of discrimination including their root causes from a gender perspective' (Resolution E/CN.4/L.59, quoted by Yuval-Davis: 194).

Yuval-Davis also argues that the debates around intersectionality do not question the relationship of the divisions but rather the relative conflation or separation of the different analytic levels. In other words intersectionality is a critique of the original triple oppression analysis that tended to pull out specific facts in isolation in order to explain the oppression of 'black women'. Yuval-Davis, who has made significant contributions in developing how this concept is used to analyse women's oppression, states:

> We argue that each social division has a different ontological basis, which is irreducible to other social divisions. However, this does not make it less important to acknowledge that, in concrete experiences of oppression, being oppressed, for example, as 'a Black person' is always constructed and intermeshed in other social divisions (for example, gender, social class, disability status, sexuality, age, nationality, immigration status, geography etc.). Any attempt to essentialise 'Blackness' or 'womanhood' or 'working classness' as specific forms of concrete oppression in additive ways inevitably conflates narratives of identity politics with descriptions of positionality as well as constructing identities within the terms of specific political projects. Such narratives often reflect hegemonic discourses of identity politics that render invisible experience of the more marginal members of that specific social category and construct an homogenized 'right way' to be its member. (2006: 195)

This book attempts to give voice to those whose life experiences are often rendered invisible. What comes through in the narratives are the subtle contradictions in terms of the challenges and defences each woman articulates towards her own culture, but also the secular state within which she lives. Lines are blurred, for example, in Chapter 3. The contributor reflects proudly on her Somali culture and then later is highly critical of the patriarchal values deeply embedded in it. Although she is aware of the contradictory picture she is presenting, her responses reveal the ambiguous position many women feel towards their heritage. The stories in Chapter 2 about FGM also reveal the less than straightforward position many women find themselves in. The contributor in this chapter gives her own story of FGM, presenting it as evidence of her gender oppression but at the same time the second woman whose story is placed alongside emphasises the importance of the practice as an expression of Somali womanhood.

Yuval-Davis (2006) compares different definitions and practical translations of intersectionality and highlights a level of confusion in its application. Intersectionality is used at times to explain structural inequalities whilst at other points or sometimes even in the same analysis also given to discuss issues of identity and personhood. As stated above, this dual application of the term can certainly be seen in the analysis of the stories recorded and presented here; women draw on differing dimensions to explain their suffering and to affirm their positive self-image and identity (chapters 3, 4, 6 and 7). What comes through in the stories is that culture, tradition and religion are not in themselves the problems, but rather in certain contexts it is the way they feed into and help to perpetuate misogynistic values that produces and sustains abusive and violent practices against women.

The most important application of intersectionality is to understand, as Essed (1993) states, incidents of 'everyday racism'. A focus on structural inequalities then enables an understanding of how the race and gender of black women shape actual experiences of domestic violence and rape, for example, differently from those of white women. Crenshaw points out the political intersectionality in relation to the manner in which both feminist and anti-racist politics have functioned in tandem to marginalise the issue of violence against women of colour (Crenshaw, 1993: 3, quoted by Yuval-Davis, 2006: 198). In order to avoid conflating different positionalities, values and identities various kinds of differences need to be incorporated into the analysis of women's experiences. Some social divisions such as class and race may be enmeshed but they should not be assumed to be reducible to each other. What is clear in the stories recorded here is that the secular state in the UK has failed to make any real impact on reversing patterns of marginalisation experienced by women. The stories told here, although clearly highlighting the misogynistic sanctioning of oppressive practices, also reveal a consistent lack of state-level support for vulnerable women. Southall Black Sisters (SBS) report that they increasingly struggle for funding:

> By the late 1990s, for a brief period, it appeared as if our struggles against domestic violence were finally achieving results following recognition by the state of the need to develop 'mature multiculturalism', an approach which necessitates the recognition of the human rights of black minority women. However, more recent developments have greatly undermined this position ... since 9/11 and the London bombings in July 2005, the state's new approach to race relations involves the implementation of a 'faith' and 'cohesion' agenda which represents the 'softer' face of its counter terrorism measures. The shift from multiculturalism to 'multi faithism' reveals a dual and contradictory approach to minority women. On the one hand, the state appears to be tackling gender-based violence, for example, forced marriage and honour crimes, although it also uses these issues to tighten immigration controls. On the other hand, it actively encourages a 'faith'-based approach which reinforces unequal gender and other power relations within minority communities. We conclude that the consequent shrinking of the secular spaces – a necessary precondition for women's struggle for freedom in the personal and public spheres – unless vigorously resisted, threatens the gains made by Asian women. This is clearly demonstrated by our campaign in 2008 against Ealing Council which sought to withdraw our funding and therefore essential services for abused minority women in the name of 'equality', 'diversity' and 'cohesion'. This experience marks a significant watershed in Asian women's struggles against those who use religion and racism to limit our freedoms. (Patel and Siddiqui, 2010: 102–03)

Patel and Siddiqui document the changing impact of government policy on the work of SBS (also summarised in Chapter 8). They begin by presenting a critique of multiculturalism, highlighting that in some respects it unintentionally but also intentionally reinforces abusive practices. This is largely because the concept was used by public servants such as social workers as an excuse not to engage with the specific abuse suffered by black minority ethnic women (see the case described by Patel and Siddiqui of Afia whose social worker refused to listen to her fears of an imminent forced marriage, pp. 105–06). By reducing a BME woman's case of abuse to a 'cultural issue' social workers can choose to ignore it on the grounds that people of different heritage have the right to live according to different values and beliefs.

In 1999 Mike O'Brien established a Home Office working group on forced marriage in response to the murder of Rukhsana Naz in 1998 by her mother and brother for refusing to stay in a forced marriage. He coined a new term, 'mature multiculturalism', and called for an end to what he described as a moral blindness when it came to the experiences of abuse suffered by BME women. For SBS this was an important moment which led to the establishment of a forced marriage unit and much greater willingness within the establishment to pursue convictions and protection for vulnerable BME women. However, the introduction of the multi-faithism agenda under the umbrella of improving community cohesion in the aftermath of 9/11 has resulted in an increase in women's vulnerability and a reversal of the positive in-roads detailed above.

> Although the state has begun to assert more clearly the view that harmful cultural practices will not be tolerated, the 'faith'-based approach contributes to a set of policies aimed at recognising and protecting religious identity, increasingly to the detriment of women's rights. In our experience, the accommodation of religious identity within state institutions, including the legal system, is undermining, albeit slowly and surreptitiously, the rights of minority women. This is illustrated by the ways in which the state appears to be toying with the demand to incorporate aspects of shariah laws (mainly in relation to the family) within the legal system, a move which is encouraged by leaders of the church and judiciary. (Patel and Siddiqui, 2010: 111)

For SBS the worrying change can be seen in the post-9/11 increases in anti-Muslim racism. In response, Muslim women have begun to come together in different ways to protect their religious identity. This in turn has resulted in groups demanding greater protection of the right to live a Muslim way of life. Patel and Siddiqui, however, assert that such demands mask the real agenda, which is to perpetuate the control of women's 'hearts, minds and bodies' (2010: 115). We are seeing a rise in faith schools, changes to dress codes to allow religious identity to be expressed and demands to apply customary religious laws instead of civil laws in governance and family affairs. All of these are shaped by patriarchal values and beliefs.

Some women whose stories are documented in this volume talk of feeling isolated and misunderstood, which adds to their suffering. The lack of detailed research into the lives of different BME women also reveals an inadequate state level reaction. Effective responses to the abuses women suffer must start with knowledge of the different ways these abuses manifest themselves. Also, more qualitative investigation is needed into why patterns of oppression remain even when activists, community leaders and government officials acknowledge they exist and actively try to end them. At points the women in this book play religion and culture against each other, placing them in convenient opposition, allowing religion to remain untainted and culture to, in Narayan's words, be condemned as the problem. This distinction is made by women internal to the cultures they write about; it is therefore much harder to critique their perspectives on the grounds of being essentialist and/or racist. In an argument I have made previously in response to Narayan's critique, I state that 'While the "death by culture approach" is orientalist and unhelpful, and distorts and simplifies the causes and consequences of domestic violence in the lives of south Asian women, Narayan is too quick to dismiss the influence of the religion-culture nexus upon women's lives' (2009: 262). The stories presented here attest to the centrality of religion and culture in women's self-analysis of harmful practices and instances of injustice. I argue that rather than remove culture completely from the picture, the analytical challenge is to retain space for religion and culture in an intersectional approach but still challenge assumptions that 'culture' somehow affects some groups of women more than others. Scholars working in the area of gender and religion have long argued that a cross-cultural perspective is needed to recognise the universality of abuses against women whilst also stressing the importance of unpacking the complexities and differentials of any case.

Links between religion, culture and tradition

Conceptually different disciplines handle religion and culture in varying ways, some, such as the study of religion and theology, treating them as separate but intrinsically interlocking categories. In contrast, disciplines such as anthropology conflate religion and culture (see Bradley, 2010). Anthropologists focus on 'culture' as a broad analytical term which encompasses religious belief, symbols and ritual practices as well as the distinctiveness of everyday behaviour, food, clothes, routine. A central part of the anthropological use of the term culture is an appreciation of tradition, closely related to notions of heritage, which are passed down through generations enabling groups to retain their distinctness and preserve an identity that in turn provides a crucial sense of who they are and what their place is in the world. Culture, religion and tradition therefore for anthropologists operate to set boundaries between people and groups; they send clear messages about how people should behave and the codes that should be conformed to.

Scholars in religious studies are much more careful to distinguish between religion and culture. Religion represents the authoritative source of truth founded often on concepts of the divine whose sacredness ensures that all that comes from this source is beyond question. Religion is often concerned to project ideas about the origins and purpose of life which then feed into culture, producing moral codes and laws to which adherents are expected to conform. Religion and culture are inextricably linked but understanding this relationship helps researchers appreciate how particular practices are justified and maintained for generations. Religion is important to many people across the globe because it forms a lens through which they see and relate to the world and provides a sense of identity and belonging. It also provides a moral code to live by and therefore impacts on decision-making processes and human actions. Religion exists in people's lives through a series of spaces, both institutional and personal. Figures of religious authority offer guidance over how to face the challenges of everyday life. Religious leaders and teachers interpret sacred texts, helping adherents translate religious values, concepts and beliefs into their lives. Religion is also a private affair. A great deal of a person's religious life occurs internally in personal dialogue with sacred images and concepts (Bradley, 2006).

Religion emerges in various places in this volume, either as a source of pride and/or guidance. Some women talk about their religious identity as central in shaping who they are. In other chapters religious spaces become important resources in women's fight against domestic violence, or social networking spaces within which support can be gained when difficult decisions need to be made. In other chapters the influence of religious leaders, even in a secular society such as the UK, becomes clear. In Chapter 5 we see that Islamic divorce proceedings require the involvement of imams who do not always act quickly to respond to women's experiences of domestic violence. The authority of religious leaders means that their actions, or lack of them, are not readily challenged either by the women concerned or members of the wider community. The authority of religious leaders is based on a claim to know and understand divine truths upon which life is built; this knowledge is rarely questioned and means that the patriarchal status quo they uphold remains largely intact generation after generation. Secular values have done little to challenge and destabilise the authority of religious leaders because they too are grounded in patriarchy and so share a common vision of gender relations.

Anthropologists regard religion as fundamentally an experiential concept, rather than one that can be understood through mapping out a series of behaviours (Angro, 2004; Bowen, 2002; Bowie, 2000; Crapo, 2003; Glaizer, 2003; Hicks, 2002; Lambek, 2002; Scupin, 1999; Whitehouse and Laiulaw, 2004). Bowie (2000) defines religion in her overview text on religion and anthropology in terms of a supernatural realm to which people look for explanations for why and how human life came to be. She describes religion as the arena through which spiritual and practical guidance is offered to people. What comes through in the stories told here is the extent to which the categories of religion and culture are often completely separated by the storyteller. This separation is deliberate, enabling the woman to provide explanation to her and others as to why specific practices of abuse are so systematic. Culture, or at least aspects of it, is labelled as the problem whilst religion, specifically a concept of God, is often described in quite radical terms as promoting gender equality (chapters 2 and 4). Religion is preserved by many, including some of the storytellers in this volume, as a sphere untainted by misogyny. As already touched upon, many aspects of religion fulfil important functions in women's lives across the globe in both secular and non-secular contexts. However, many religious teachers clearly promote male dominance and female submissiveness which renders women vulnerable to violence. Religious teachings, according to Asad (1992), gain legitimacy because they are claimed to emanate from a divine source of truth beyond reproach. Asad highlights the links between religion and power. He argues that religious symbols are not only intimately linked to social life but also support or oppose the dominant political power. His views resonate with those scholars positioned at a macro level, for example in international relations and politics. Reychler and Paffenholz (2000) argue that faith often presents itself as a soft power, shaping discourses that describe how the world should be, driving people to act according to that vision. Anthropologists such as Asad support this view, claiming that religion shapes how people perceive their role in life, thus influencing actions. He acknowledges that religious beliefs and practices are not static but change with history, but as many of the accounts given in this volume reveal, religion also acts to preserve male power.

The authority of religion is ensured through the adaptation of beliefs and practices in order to suit the needs of a new emerging order. In the context of the stories given here, religious beliefs, and specifically the authority of religious teachings, are drawn upon by women to challenge the oppressive effects of particular practices. However, scholars working within the field of gender and religion argue that this separation between religion and culture conveniently allows oppression to be attributed to the cultural sphere and ignores the extent to which religious teachings endorse and protect a patriarchal ideology that represents the foundations of gender-based violence. Gender therefore also needs to be added to the lens through which the cultural practices explored in this volume are analysed:

Religion and gender are not simply two parallel categories that function independently of each other; they are mutually embedded within each other in all religions, suffusing all religious worlds and experiences. It is because [of this] deep hidden embeddedness that gender is sometimes so difficult to identify and separate out from other aspects of religions until one's own consciousness is trained into making a gender critical turn. (King, 2005: 3299)

Once we see religion as gendered, the next step is to examine its far-reaching effects on wider society and human relationships. King argues, moreover, that religions operate in very similar ways and create environments that support the elitism and authority of men over women even in societies that might regard themselves as largely secular. The relationships between religious traditions and misogynistic ideals, which in turn sustain an often hostile environment for women, have been identified across all religious traditions (King, 1995; Young, 1995; Young, Sharma and Young, 1991; King and Beattie, 2004). In the case of Hinduism, explored in Chapter 7 in the context of dowry, its patriarchal values produce and sustain a preference for sons and male succession, which clearly privileges the male subject, whereas women have been designated the role of looking after them. This gendered vision of social/human relationships that emerges from son-preference renders women inferior to the authority of men and renders them vulnerable to male control. Various mechanisms have emerged to ensure women comply with the patriarchal foundations of their society; for example, female infanticide, domestic violence, bride-burning and harassment all operate to enforce and/or perpetuate the idea that women are of less value than men. In arguing the role religion plays in sustaining and promoting women's inferiority I quote in Bradley (2010: 104) the following passage taken from a widely read Hindu epic, The Ramayana by Tulsidas: 'If women became independent, it would lead to evil ... The drum, the village fool, the shudras, animals, women ... all these are fit to be beaten.'

The direct legitimising of violence as a way of controlling and disciplining women is self-evident in this passage; so too is the lowly position in which women are held. As already stated, religion alone cannot explain women's position but should form one dimension in an intersectional explanation (see also Bradley, 2010). In Chapter 7 it is suggested that the chain leading to dowry begins in Hinduism with son preference, heterosexual marriage and wifely submission, upon which modern dowry practices feed in many parts of India, leaving women vulnerable to dowry-related violence and also other forms of violence. Religion plays a part in securing the first links of this chain and this is clear from textual analysis of Hindu epics, for instance, and also through anthropological studies of the role of women in Hindu society. Cultural practices such as dowry and FGM arguably 'feed' from 'traditions', which aim to ensure that male needs and desires define and dominate women's lives and roles (see also Knott, 1996). Particular dimensions of religion that promote and protect patriarchy, elevating male authority and superiority underpinned by wifely submission, have helped to construct and create a social environment in which female oppression flourishes. The stories told here in different ways reveal examples of the embedded gender ideology that clearly supports abuse and marginalisation of women. Once again we see that the secular nature of the state makes little difference to the existence of practices and traditions that support patriarchy and indeed seems to help practices such as dowry continue virtually unnoticed.

Narayan's work makes a significant contribution in encouraging researchers to be more sensitive and self-critical in their writings on dowry. Particularly white, middle-class scholars need to both challenge their own motivations and also ensure their representations of other women are founded on what they witness and hear women articulating for themselves and not on their own exotic imaginings. Without being informed by face-to-face dialogues, researchers cannot be confident they understand the processes that produce dowry and the violence often emerging because of it. Without the kind of close research such as that presented here, the full complexity of how male superiority manages to weave itself into the very fabric of society will remain unclear. Those few sources that exist on domestic violence in the UK do not consider how patriarchy is able to maintain itself with the help of culture, tradition and religion. Although patriarchy is seen as the foundation of women's oppression, its roots – beyond analysis that highlights that different social systems across the globe favour men –

are left relatively unexamined. While activists/researchers express frustration at the seemingly impenetrable nature of the patriarchal gender ideology responsible for harmful practices and/or the consequences of male dominance, I argue that the role played by religion and culture in sanctioning patriarchy can in part help us to understand the embeddedness of them. Part of the reluctance to include religion and culture in an intersectional approach relates to theories of secularism that argued that religion would diminish as a more scientific and rational way of viewing the world took hold. The world free of religion described by secular theorists has failed to materialise (see Beyer, 1994; Beyer and Beaman, 2007). Scholars now argue (King, 1995; Bradley and Tomalin, 2009) that we must return to religion and culture to help us explain the emergence of more virulent forms of fundamentalist religion that have provoked a resurgence in conservative views of gender.

A balance, therefore, needs to be found that understands the ways in which religion and culture weave together to support a chain of patriarchy but that does not reduce gender discrimination and its manifestations, such as dowry practices and female circumcision, solely to religious or cultural causes.

This study not only seeks to offer closer insights into how and why these practices flourish but also reveals how the reconstruction of the categories of religion and culture have enabled women to find answers and thereby at least make sense of why they have suffered abuse. This process of reconstructing the relationship between religion and culture also becomes part of a process of identity formation in which the women present themselves not as victims of culture but as active agents whose religious identity and sense of morality guides them to act, resist and cope with tough experiences. The thread that links the book together then is the analysis of how religion and culture, alongside other dimensions, are understood and emerge through the life stories as part of the explanation and also condemnation of practices harmful to women.

Filling a gap

There are no books that directly cover the breadth of this volume, both in terms of regional and themetic coverage, or that attempt to record so many different personal testimonies. There are a number of texts that explore cultural issues covering some of the same ground in terms of exploring how personhood and identity are reconfigured post-migration and how this changes through the generations. As already stated, most research centres on the south Asia diaspora, for example Brown (2006), Kalra and Sayyid (2006), and Puwar and Raghuram (2003). Although fewer, there are some texts looking at aspects of the African diaspora, for example Clark Hine, Keaton and Small (2009), and Mercer, Page and Evans (2008). Also, with a specific gendered focus, Byfield, Denzer and Morrison (2010) explore how cultural and historical change in the Caribbean and Nigerian hinterland have impacted on women's lives. These are all edited volumes and either have a broad regional focus, talking about a global diaspora, or they look at how the diaspora responds to specific developmental issues. Recent interest has emerged in exploring how charitable giving to the 'home' country enables members of the diaspora to retain some influence over local decision-making.

This volume is distinct from these cited texts because, as already stated, it is founded on ethnographic oral narratives which are then used to reflect on how women from African and south Asian backgrounds reinterpret and reformulate their identities. The stories also show how BME women challenge negative assumptions and misrepresentations made by 'others' in the UK. They show how they challenge structures and practices that repress them internal to their culture. In doing this it draws out competing and ambiguous perceptions of culture and the role of these practices in preserving and promoting cultural values. Many of these stories disclose instances of gender-based violence, specifically FGM, domestic violence and, in Chapter 7, forced marriage. The wider literature on these issues can be divide into four main categories: *legal or policy briefing publications* documenting the legislative position and prevalence in regard to each practice (for example, Skaire and Jefferson, 2005; Heaton, McCallum and Razi, 2009; and Jordon, 2006); secondly, *texts with a health perspective* examining the medical implications of certain cultural practices such as FGM (for example, Karaya, 2003; Lochat, 2004; and Momoh, 2005); thirdly, *autobiographical or biographical accounts of one person's experience of a specific practice* such as Al-Shaykh (2009), Alexander (2005) and Mai (2007); lastly, *feminist texts or those written by activists and/or members of an NGO*, most famously, for example, the work of Fatima Mernissi (1992).

Rather than covering only one aspect or instance of gender-based violence, this study covers head-on a variety of practices, depending on what those women participating in the research wished to talk about. It also combines personal reflections with policy advice and critical analysis of current literature and research. *Women, Violence and Tradition* is intended to represent a snapshot, however small, of the concerns and experiences of black minority ethnic women in Britain. It is intended to give some insights into the importance or not of religion, culture and tradition in shaping identity and in forming the lens through which women view the world, form their relationships and perceptions of others and make sense of their experiences.

Summary of chapters

Chapter 1 reviews the methodological approach of life histories used in most of the research for this study. In this chapter the benefits of this method is considered as a means of accessing sensitive and holistic insight into women's lives. It also gives more detail on how the stories have been analysed, drawing on the work of Liz Kelly who uses a continuum to highlight the continued presence of patriarchy at the heart of all cases of abuse, which then intersects with an array of other factors. For example, class and ethnicity shape distinct experiences and contexts in which violence and/or oppression occur. In this chapter the researchers themselves talk about and share their own personal journeys which they embarked upon as a result of doing this research. Through recording their reflections it becomes clear how distinct the life histories approach is as a means of facilitating critical and personal self-evaluation.

In **Chapter 2** Isha Abulkadir tells the stories of two generations of Somali women, all of whom have been circumcised. The chapter reviews the literature on this practice and highlights the concentration of research on the medical and legal implications of female circumcision and considers the anthropological explanations behind its prevalence. The stories reveal different viewpoints and responses, but all agree that the practice involves immense suffering; however, only the youngest woman is adamant that it is wrong and must be ended. The stories also reveal how the practice is woven into Somali tradition and represents, for two of the women, a significant rite in a woman's life that helps mark the transition to adult identity, facilitating an understanding of her place in the world. This chapter also at points stands back from the stories and considers how the personal experiences of practices such as FGM are used to guide and inform activism. It then considers how a life/oral history approach could be further developed in the context of community development. This chapter will contain the responses of those practitioners, activists and feminists who work on this issue. How do activists approach FGM? How successful are community groups in recording this practice and responding to it? What feeling do they hold as to whether this practice has increased or decreased in recent times? What is sustaining the practice into the next generation of women?

In **Chapter 3** Ebyan Ahmed focuses on the importance of Somali marriage practices as opportunities for women to celebrate their culture and meet with others across generations, sharing concerns and joys. The stories reveal the process of socialisation girls undergo through tales about their future marriage. The women talk of the expectations pinned to this rite of passage and the excitement felt as girls look forward to this defining moment when they become wives and fully-fledged women. The stories contrast these joyous expectations and celebration of cultural heritage against the harsh realities of marriage that many young Somali wives have had to adjust to. The tension between their desire to remain independent and pursue careers, and the expectations of their husbands who want them to conform to the traditional image of a Somali wife, are evident. Navigating a path through these competing ideas of women's role and purpose, as the author's reflections reveal, cause real anguish and trauma.

Chapter 4, written by Esline Dzumbunu, documents stories of domestic violence among women of the Zimbabwean diaspora community. This chapter focuses on stories from one specific community, examining the domestic context in which violence emerges. It offers two narratives: one account is given of a woman's experiences of domestic violence whilst still in Zimbabwe; the other is a young newly-wed woman's tale of the violence she suffered at the hand of her husband shortly after arriving in the UK. These stories have much in common and highlight the extent to which patriarchal values woven into cultural ideals about gender and family life have caused and enabled these instances of abuse. This chapter also draws out through the accounts the importance of religion, specifically in this case Christianity, as offering both the space and also the language to help women confront violence in their daily lives. The second story, about Mary, reveals how her life in the UK did not provide her with the opportunities she had hoped for: she felt isolated and marginalised, and it was only when she found the courage to leave and was able to access support through a local church network that she was able to begin a better life.

In **Chapter 5** Noorjahan Begum sensitively shares accounts of marriage and divorce given by three women from the Bangladeshi community in Tower Hamlets. The author did not expect to find that the life histories she recorded would all contain violence. The tales reveal how hard it is for a Bengali woman to leave an abusive marriage and how in the first instance blame is placed with her. All the women whose stories are documented in this chapter stayed in their violent marriages for longer then perhaps they wanted. They were advised by community and religious leaders to stay and try to work things through; the violence they suffered was not seen as of particular significance. The stories therefore reveal the extent to which violence against women is legistimised and supported by patriarchal religious and cultural values that hold women responsible for the success of their marriage. However, this bleak picture is contradicted to some extent by one of the women describing their financial independence once divorced because of the marriage practice of *mehr* which ensured that they had money set aside in case they needed to leave their husband. The stories also reveal something of the internal support network that women can access, and although it is not always quick to respond to violence, in each case the woman has started a new life free from violence.

Chapter 6, entitled 'Transnational Accounts of Dowry and Caste', is written by Charlenie Naik. In it she explores how dowry is a highly contested practice which has provoked significant reaction and campaigning among Indian feminists and activists. This chapter presents case examples of how dowry continues to be practised by high-caste Hindu families living in the diaspora communities of Manchester and Leeds. These testimonies suggest that the practice is supported by men and women and reflects their status as *Brahmin* Hindus. The way in which dowry is observed is documented in the stories which also emphasise that the women themselves view dowry as a degrading and misogynistic practice. It seems clear that although dowry has always been a part of Hindu life in Britain, the UK government has consistently failed to recognise the links between dowry and dowry abuses. Although the women whose stories are documented here do not talk about abuse, they do share their anguish and the constant tension that they live with as they try to challenge and navigate around strict patriarchal expectations which dowry symbolises.

Chapter 7, written by Sana Khilji and titled 'The Big Taboo: Stories of Premarital Relationships', cleverly combines honest and open accounts provided by two BME women who entered into premarital relationships. The accounts talk of the need for these relationships to be kept secret and of the guilt and shame they felt in having to do so. The chapter also interviews a Pakistani father who fears that his daughters will be led astray by the temptations of the secular society they live in but also accepts that he must let them have relationships with men 'as long as the line is not crossed'. His more liberal views contradict the image of fierce autocratic Muslim fathers yet he still defends the traditional patriarchal values he was raised with. The contrasting views of the three informants in this chapter highlight the misconceptions internal to families over how parents might react to premarital relationships and suggests a more relaxed approach is emerging over time, but also reinforces research that highlights the extent to which Islamic culture and values are still centred on the behavour of women. Navigating culture, tradition and secular opportunities is the cause of a great deal of stress for the young women in this chapter. Although the tensions and clashes revealed in this chapter are well known to many, the voices of young women are rarely documented directly, and these stories give a very real sense of the anguish and pain many go through as they try to balance competing sets of values.

Chapter 8, written by Hannana Siddiqui, follows the lives of four women from black and minority ethnic communities who have experienced gender-based violence, namely domestic violence, so called 'honour'-based violence, forced marriage and dowry abuse. It looks at the extremes as two cases resulted in murder or suicide but it also examines women's experiences of routine abuse which, if unchallenged, can escalate to tragedy. It places the lives of three women in the wider context of the BME women's movement and the gains and losses they have made in challenging violence against BME women in a world where we witness a global recession and massive public sector cuts, a rise in religious fundamentalism and identity, the growth of the far right and 'rights for whites' demands, misguided social cohesion and anti-terror policies post-9/11 and a strong feminist women's movement fighting against violence against women and girls as one of its prime objectives. In particular, it looks at the work of a BME women's organisation, Southall Black Sisters, which has led the way in raising and addressing these issues in relation to the needs of BME, particularly south Asian women, for over thirty years.

The **Conclusion** pulls out overarching themes and experiences that run throughout the volume and attempts to theorise what the stories reveal about how the state supports or fails to support the aspirations of BME women. In the conclusion the following questions will be explored:

- How can this research and the life history approach be used by community activists and organisations?

- What do these stories tell us about the lives of ethnic minority women in Britain?
- What type of feminisms emerge from this data?
- How should the policy world and community activists respond?

The conclusion attempts to leave readers with a practical focus and sense of how the kind of qualitative research contained in this study can in fact feed into and help create sensitive and meaningful interventions.

1
Researching Stories

Introduction

The methodology adopted by the researchers in the seven chapters to follow is the life or oral histories approach. This method literally involves asking people to orally recount either the whole story of their life or a period of it or even one particular experience. The approach begins with the researcher/story-recipient asking the informant/ storyteller to, in whatever language they feel comfortable with, share with them their life experiences. From here on I will use the term 'recipient' to refer to the researcher who has recorded the life experiences of the informant, called the 'storyteller'. The terms 'recipient' and 'storyteller' reflect the relationship at the heart of this methodology.

This approach seeks to destabilise the power relations between the person who shares their experience and the researcher who records and later analyses it, producing a written account for public consumption. The start is gentle and control is given to the storyteller to set the pace and tone of their own narrative. The storyteller decides what experiences they will share with the recipient and what they will hold back. This approach enables the storyteller to ease into the process of recounting her often personal experiences. After a time the storyteller often settles into a pace they are comfortable with and as they feel more secure with the situation so they feel more able and willing to share with the recipient personal insights.

As the stories recounted in this volume reveal, the process often begins with the storyteller offering the recipient some background details into the context of their lives. The recipient has asked that the storyteller begins with this detail as it not only gives a sense of the context of a person's life, but also enables the process to start in a less intrusive place. As the stories shared here contest, it does not take long before a more personal and emotive narrative emerges. The women who share their lives in this volume are reassured by the presence of a recipient who is also female and from the same culture and community. It is naive to assume that sharing a gendered and cultural identity and living within the same community will remove all differences, but it does, as the storytellers in this research claim, make them feel more at ease and confident that their recipient will empathise with the more personal and harrowing aspects of their story.

The process of hearing and recording life histories cannot easily be squeezed into a limited time frame and the recipients have to let narratives emerge gently. This at times is difficult: when the storyteller seems to be lost in seemingly irrelevant detail, the recipient will find the urge to interject and redirect the storyteller hard to resist. In the stories recorded here the recipients have at times interjected and prompted the storyteller to refocus or delve into another area of their life history. These prompts have been necessary in order to preserve the key objective behind this volume which is to make visible BME women's experiences of balancing and expressing their cultural heritage within the secular backdrop of the UK. In seeking out these experiences the study pursues an underlying political objective to create a platform for BME women to resist aspects of their culture and tradition; also to challenge the ways in which they have been misrepresented and negatively presented by individuals and state agencies outside of their immediate diaspora. This politicised intention, some might argue, compromises the way in which recipients have employed the life histories approach; however, the personal insights shared in the pages to come would not have emerged without it.

The stories shared have been edited, although as much of the narratives as possible have been included. The stories were all collected in the storytellers' first language and so have been translated by the recipients. Each story focuses on a specific practice or experience covering between them marriage, divorce, female genital mutilation

(FGM), dowry, domestic violence and pre-marriage relationships. From the outset the recipients made it clear that they wanted the storytellers to focus on a specific practice or experience but asked them to begin at whatever point in their life seemed appropriate to them; some therefore begin with childhood, others much later into adulthood and married life. What these stories share is an underlying narrative of patriarchy, which in some cases has led to violence. In other accounts, although no violence was experienced by the storyteller, they still relay feelings of confusion and anguish. As recounted in the Introduction, for many of the contributors the intention was not to write about violence or even negative and/or emotionally traumatic experiences, yet all the stories contain either narratives of abuse or fear of it, or accounts of tension and confusion over how to navigate around patriarchal traditions and values. The extent to which the narratives draw out these tensions and instances of blatant abuse surprised and shocked the recipients and, as their own testaments reveal, have made them more determined to continue the project of raising awareness of the pressures and abuse many BME women face in their daily lives.

This chapter will begin with a summary of the life history methodology and present expansive discussion about the analytical frame used to contextualise and engage with the stories. Included in this discussion on how to analyse life histories is consideration of the ethical difficulties this approach poses. Although the recipients' experiences of doing this research are woven throughout this methodology chapter, the final section documents more directly the personal and professional journeys they went through.

Oral histories approach and ethical considerations

Storytelling is a natural part of the human experience. Human beings communicate meaning through talk. Oral historians have harnessed this tradition of transmitting knowledge and created an important research technique that allows the expression of voice. While storytelling has a deep history, the adaptation of this human process into a legitimated research method is relatively new. Oral history was established in 1948 as a modern technique for historical documentation when Columbia University historian

Allan Nevins began recording the memoirs of persons significant in American life. (North American Oral History Association, as quoted by Thomson, 1998, p. 581)

Although for some time researchers, in particular anthropologists and sociologists, have conducted research on oral traditions, the methodology of oral history or life history research has emerged as a distinct way of collecting in-depth data. This approach enables much closer insights into the complexities of people's life experiences than other techniques allow. There are no short cuts in this approach and story-recipients must be prepared to spend extended periods of time with their storytellers. In the context of this volume all the authors are part of or in some way connected to the communities they write about. This already established relationship with their storytellers has enabled, to some degree, a lengthy getting-to-know and trust period to be circumvented.

As stated at the start of this chapter, oral history research is essentially a collaboration between a recipient, who records the words of the storyteller, and a storyteller, who provides the account. The way in which these stories are presented and analysed presents interpretive challenges. In this volume the placing of stories side by side is in itself an act of interpretation, even when no analytical narrative is woven between them. The reader is encouraged to draw out differences and similarities and 'imagine' whose situation is worse, and think about how they may act in the same position. The conclusions readers may draw about the lives of the women whose stories they read could well harmfully reinforce essentialist stereotypes. To guard against this is the responsibility of the author, to whom the storyteller has entrusted their personal narrative. Once more, the positioning of the authors inside the communities from which they have drawn their stories means they also have their own experiences and knowledge to guide them in the process of representing the lives of women with whom they share at least some commonalities. Some of the chapters in this volume combine aspects of an oral history approach with qualitative interviewing. In some cases the recipient struggled to get their informants to embrace the idea of being a storyteller and had to use questions as prompts. The objectives of this study were such that the researchers also needed to focus on specific periods of their informants' lives or on isolated experiences or practices. This need to circumvent the story to identify moments or instances in a sense contradicts the essence of the oral histories approach, but what emerges is a fluid combination of techniques. The recipients/authors move between approaches dependent on the feelings of their storytellers, and have facilitated an open process ensuring that important insights into the life experiences of BME women have been captured (see Harding and Gabriel, 2004).

In the final section some of the authors reflect on the journey they have been through in writing their chapters. These stories are self-reflective and reveal what they learnt about themselves and their communities as a result of using the life histories approach. The researchers' reflections are filled with anxiety, not least because as the process went on they increasingly realised that they had responsibilities towards their storytellers. The recipients had responsibility to ensure the narratives shared would be written up accurately and sensitively. They did not want to misrepresent the life of any of the women who have displayed such courage in sharing deeply personal experiences. In some instances recipients became concerned that the literal retelling of a woman's story was making the storyteller seem like a victim, crippled by passivity, accepting abuse as part of her everyday life. The story recipients felt concerned about the kind of homogenous assumptions that may materialise from what appeared – on first hearing some life stories – to be the passive acceptation of abuse. Concerns were also raised which have been discussed in the Introduction, that the images created of Bengali, Somali, Indian and Zimbabwean women could help to perpetuate stereotypes of BME women as victims. At the same time we hoped these stories would sensitively convey the complexity of how and why each woman confronted her hardship. We hoped to be true to the intersectional approach and ensure that culture and/or religion did not disproportionally come through as the dominant factor but that the array of interlocking dimensions that construct each woman's experiences should be conveyed. Whilst listening to one of her storytellers Ebyan recalls that she was forced to think 'why'? Why is this woman's narrative endorsing her as a victim devoid of agency? In seeking out answers to this 'why' question Ebyan looks at the wider secular environment in which her informant lives. She considers her isolation and the lack of support available, the lack of alternatives. This woman is not a victim but has been forced to accept her situation because there are no viable alternatives. The storyteller in Ebyan's Chapter 3 accepts that conformity to the patriarchal norm of her culture is necessary. In fact her conformity could be understood as a strategy she has reluctantly and consciously accepted.

Noorjahan's stories of divorce reveal a pattern of violence, but the first two stories are contrasted against the last which reveals a supportive family that jumps in to restore their daughter and grandson's life after many years of physical and psychological abuse. This is an important narrative to include because it offers optimism but also highlights that despite the overwhelming tales of violence, in the end the solutions can be and are sought internal to the diaspora community. Highlighting and making more visible these supportive responses challenges those who assume certain cultures do not offer women any escape routes from domestic violence.

Many stories in this volume highlight the lack of in-between spaces; BME women often remain loyal to their cultural heritage and so do not want to completely step into a secular space outside of their cultural and religious community. This reluctance is often due to fear that they may experience an even greater degree of abuse, racial as well as gendered. Yet at the same time most of the women whose lives are documented in this volume do want to experience greater freedom and make decisions for themselves about the lives they wish to lead, which fundamentally involves a life without violence, abuse and oppression. Many of the stories told here reveal a lack of space between culture, tradition and the secular values of the state, preventing BME women from restructuring their identities on their terms without the pressures of having to pacify the competing ideologies of secularism versus tradition.

The oral/life histories approach when used by the recipients to record information from within their own family can reveal insights previously unknown to them. Esline growing up knew of her mother's experiences of domestic violence. She knew her father had turned violent but she did not expect to also hear that her grandmother had endured a violent marriage. This repeated pattern of domestic violence shocked her and caused her to reflect on constructions of Zimbabwean masculinities, and to ask questions about whether there is something present in the socialisation and cultural environment of Zimbabwean men that causes at least some men to feel violence is a legitimate means to control women. However, at the same time she recognises her responsibility to project a balanced view and not to give the impression that Zimbabwean men, more than others, are innately violent. She also wanted to send the message that there are many ways of being a man in Zimbabwean culture and to open up this discussion so that violence against women is condemned more publically within her diaspora community.

Given the ethical pitfalls involved in representing the lives of others, what then is the value of this approach? As the stories recounted here attest, this approach enables us to present the complex world BME women inhabit in the UK diapsoras. It also enables us close insight into how traditional values have transplanted themselves through migration and live on even in a secular state such as the UK. Understanding the challenges these traditional values present for women today can help us position sensitive challenges towards those aspects of tradition that perpetuate gender violence and oppression and offer more effective support.

Analytic frame and ethical precautions

The documenting of life histories is not in itself enough to constitute an original contribution; these stories have to be contextualised and analysed. Reading the chapters side by side reveals overlapping and repeated themes; pulling these out reveals common failures and inadequacies in the state's responses to the problems BME women face. These common themes also point towards underlying structural constraints and inequalities that render women inferior to men and therefore vulnerable to abuse and control. Kelly (2005) describes a continuum of gender-based violence that is a useful and critical way of analysing all instances of violence against women (not only BME women). The concept of a continuum enables each experience to be unravelled according to the specific mix of factors that culminated in that woman's abuse. The extent to which cultural and/or religious values and beliefs are visibly responsible will differ. Patriarchy represents the consistent foundation for all instances; variations occur only in the exact nature of the violent abuse suffered and the mechanisms through which it occurs. The analysis in this volume attempts to take things one step further and delve into the factors that enable patriarchy to retain dominance in each woman's life. In other words, why is it that despite the evidence, activism and public condemnation of violence against women that patriarchy still retains its pervasive presence cross-culturally in women's lives? The answer lies in the desire of a few to maintain power and authority, but the means through which this is achieved remains hard to expose. In other words, to remove violence against women requires the removal of patriarchy and this can only happen when the elite are finally prepared to relinquish power.

The stories documented here reveal the different ways that patriarchal oppression asserts itself and constrains the life opportunities of BME women. Whilst patriarchy affects the lives of all women, many BME women have additional dimensions that come together to construct their specific experiences of exclusion, racism and abuse. This volume pursues a feminist agenda to both raise the visibility of minority women but also to challenge the specific structural inequalities they face. Many of the recipients did not necessarily at the start of the process call themselves feminist, being wary of how that label is received and interpreted in wider society, often with hostility. However, as Esline in particular articulated, after listening to women tell their stories and reading those collected by the other authors, she became much more direct in not only calling herself a feminist but also an activist.

Esline documents her journey through the research process as a gradual awakening to parts of her own family story that she previously had no knowledge of. The new version of her childhood and specifically the details her mother shared about the breakdown of her marriage provoked a consciousness change in Esline. At one point she declares 'I now call myself a feminist; I think I have always been one but now I realise it.' Part of this awareness comes out of the increased research capacity she has gained through this process. She, as with the other researchers, has a new language and confidence to draw on to explain their responses to life experiences, and through which to communicate them, but also to position their practical intentions. The term *praxis* has been helpful in terms of offering the story-recipients a way of explaining and justifying what they are doing. *Praxis* denotes the relationship between research and activism and is an attempt to limit the extent of abstract theorising (see Tomalin, 2009). In the Introduction Ebyan shared her uncomfortable feelings listening to a woman's story about a difficult marriage she felt she could not leave. Ebyan felt responsible for ensuring her storyteller did not come across in the text as a passive, weak victim. This concern stirred other questions, around the end purpose of this research. At a midway point we spent time talking about the objective of the collective research the volume represents. The work is intended to bridge a gap between research and practice and much of the literature reviewed in the Introduction is written by those who straddle this divide. The chapter written by Hannana also highlights the importance of demonstrating the positive value of this research.

Researchers' reflections

All research processes represent journeys which themselves can be retold as stories. The retelling of my researchers' experiences of collecting life histories for this volume reveals how, for each of them, this process has provoked considerable introspection and self-reflection, much of it painful – but all agree it has been worth it. I interviewed some of the researchers, both collectively and individually. I asked them to reflect on what they had learnt through the research process both about themselves but also in relation to the technical aspects of using a life histories approach. I began with the authors of chapters 2 and 4 who both describe themselves as African first-generation migrants. Isha migrated from Somalia when she was twelve and Esline from Zimbabwe in her twenties. Isha began in her session with Esline by stating: 'Not everyone thinks the way you do; people don't talk about it; in hearing other peoples' stories you reflect on your own, imagining what life may be like for others.' Immediately she highlights how reflective the process of life history research is. In listening to and documenting the life histories of others she was forced to evaluate aspects of her own.

Esline reflects on the importance of her own positioning: she knew the women whose lives she documents in her chapter. She stated that 'we would not have got these stories if we hadn't known them'. Isha agreed that 'it took a while for people to trust me; the space in which the interviews took place was important. Each woman had to feel safe in the environment in which she then shared insights into her life.' One of her life histories was collected with the woman's husband present; he often interjected and added to the woman's narrative on circumcision, ensuring a male perspective was heard. Although his presence was frustrating to Isha, she acknowledged that the woman would not speak without him there. Her husband wanted it to be documented that circumcision negatively affects men. It was unclear why and how he felt this to be the case, but this was his view. Interestingly the presence of the husband did not prevent the woman from sharing the intimate details of her circumcision experience; this challenges assumptions that women don't speak about these matters in front of men and suggests that at least in some marriages men and women share openly their feelings about cultural and religious practices.

On hearing this woman detail the physical problem FGM caused her at the point of childbirth – the pain and suffering, the prolonged agonising labour resulting in a caesarian – Isha became emotional and was forced to project forward to a time when she will have children. As a young newly married woman it may not be immediate but it is her intention to have children; she was made to confront, in this story, the realities of what that experience may bring – and she cried again thinking about it.

In this interview both Esline and Isha talked about how listening to the stories of others provoked a therapeutic journey for each of them

– one in which much focus fell on childhood memories. For Isha, much time has been spent thinking about her relationship with her parents. She told me her story, of being a young four year old when she heard the moment at which her father divorced her mother. Her mother had wanted the divorce after Isha's father had married a second wife whom he made it clear he loved; their marriage had been arranged. Following the divorce Isha's father said he wanted custody of her and her younger brother. They then went to live with her grandmother, and her mother went to live in Saudi with her mother. It was whilst under the care of her grandmother that she was circumcised; although her father claimed he was against it he said there was nothing he could do given that he had essentially handed parental authority over to his mother.

Esline talks about how writing the life history of her mother filled in some of the missing gaps in her life. It also helped her to explain aspects of her makeup, her defensiveness and fierce self-reliance. She states that this research process has '[forced me] to face my own issues. I cried a lot mainly for what could have been while I was growing up, what I missed out on because of my father's violence and my mother's decision to leave him and start again.' She explained a little more: 'Mum had to work away a lot; we were sent to boarding school because there was nowhere else to go. We did not see her much; she had to keep travelling, selling things to raise the money to keep us at school. We missed having a mother; we lost a father, although it was better and safer without him; we effectively lost both parents for a period of our lives and we will never get that back.'

Both Esline and Isha spontaneously began to discuss the impact of their respective African heritage. Isha said that 'as migrants and Africans we have a lot in common'. They both talked of how in both Zimbabwean and Somali culture showing emotions was seen as a sign of weakness. They talked about how they had rarely if ever shared with their parents and siblings how they felt about events, and they both seemed sad to think of this. Esline stated that the process of asking her mother to share her life story gave them both the opportunity to express their emotional memories of their lives in Zimbabwe. Esline said, 'I wish I had heard my mother's story earlier; it helps to explain a lot of things.' Esline then tried to share her mother's life story with her younger sister but she did not want to hear it – she did not want to open the emotional wound of the past.

For Isha, thinking and writing about her own story of circumcision caused her to also revisit the feelings of emotional instability she experienced as a child being moved from one house to another, from her biological mother to her grandmother, to her father and his new wife who then became her stepmother. Esline recounts how in adulthood during a return trip to Zimbabwe she went with her mother to her father's village to see him. Her father looked at her and referred to her as an 'older woman ... he did not see me as his daughter, there was no connection, no love'. She then went on to say, 'You know he never came to look for us. Why? Why did he never try to find us? Did he not care?' She recounted how on this return trip her father's current wife killed a chicken in honour of her, which is more than anyone else in her father's family did. Esline ponders, 'I don't know how she managed to stay with him for so long. He was violent towards her. She didn't have any children. She had nowhere to go; at least my mother escaped.'

I ended my conversation with Isha and Esline by asking them what surprised them about the process. They both agreed that they had not expected it to provoke this level of self-reflection. Esline observed, 'I have cried a lot, more than I would have ever expected; it has been a sad experience but one that has made me even more determined to make a difference – this book should make a difference.' Isha agreed, acknowledging that she too had shed many tears through this process and confronted sadness, loss and fear for her future. Isha also in response to my question stated that 'the stories and reflections all link together; that's the whole point of this book. The experiences of marriage, divorce, cross-cultural relationships, circumcision, violence, all weave together in ways that I would never have expected.'

I finally asked, *What difference does migration make to women's lives?* They replied that 'in many ways things become worse, women become more isolated, find it even harder to talk about the things they would like to change in their lives. Practices such as FGM and domestic violence continue here. Many Somali parents continue to take their children abroad to be circumcised and if they can't afford this they get it done here.'

Noorjahan's reflections on her chapter are similar; she talked about how in writing the chapter it threw up many issues which she had not addressed. She reflects: 'I didn't see my storytellers as victims but the process of writing highlighted how much strength they needed to survive. Coming to the end of the writing I realised just how many emotions I pushed to the back of my mind. Reading the stories again I became angry and wanted to shout. I also became cross at myself for not acting to help women sooner.' She also reflected on the involvement the state had in Nadia's case, through the social services. She recounted how Nadia told her that a social worker had contacted her after her husband had been arrested and taken into custody following a particularly violent outburst. The social worker had said that she would need to place her son on the at risk register and closely monitor the situation, although she acknowledged that Nadia was not to blame – this was simply the procedure as the child was still considered vulnerable if living in a continuing environment of violence. Nadia said this experience deterred her from involving the police again as she feared that her son could be taken or that people in her community would begin to view the involvement of social services as an indication of her inability to mother. Noorhajan said she had thought about Nadia's responses and observed that 'social service involvement in my community is taken as a reflection of your mothering; Nadia's decision to leave meant she became a better mother but in my community if you leave you are also labelled a bad mother; this made me angry, it is so unjust'. This reflection highlights the extent to which women have very little choice; whatever they do they risk the spotlight being placed on their abilities to perform their traditional role. She also highlighted that in addition to violence operating as a mechanism to ensure women comply, the tactic of slandering also acts to ensure a similar end. Some women, more than men, in the Bengali community are frequently subjected to public slander during which their character and honour are questioned. Slanders are often made through word of mouth, but can also involve newspaper advertisements publicising in print the dubious nature of particular women. Noorjahan noted that 'slander is a means of control; a woman finds herself labelled as having something wrong with her and will find it very difficult to move past a violent marriage'.

She also reflects on the immense pressure for women to submit to their husbands. Submissiveness is highly valued among the Bengali community to such an extent that 'Bengali women from home in Bangladesh are thought of as favourable wife material because they won't cause trouble and can be used and abused.' Noorjahan reflects on a continuous cycle of isolation experienced by young Bengali brides and carried through into their adulthood, as the first narrative in her chapter shows. Nothing much has happened to challenge or reverse these experiences. Noorjahan ends her reflections with the statement, 'This research has opened my eyes – my storytellers changed their situations and I hope that reading these stories will help others follow a similar path that takes them to freer and more fulfilled lives. The process of change is slow but possible.'

Ebyan's concerns have already been touched on in the Introduction to this volume. She has been worried about misrepresenting 'her culture' and these concerns, she explains, have heightened in the post-9/11 period. Ebyan spoke about a real shift in the level of scrutiny outsiders have subjected her to. She feels more conscious of people's stares and their judgments as she travels through public spaces. She feels for Muslim women: the veil has become the focus of misrepresentation and distortion and this makes her feel uncomfortable. As people stare at her dress she feels they are making assumptions about her life, the oppression she must suffer. She wanted through her chapter to dispel this view, but at the same time, as with most of us, there remain elements of her life that she would like to alter. She has found it hard to maintain the delicate balance between highlighting the problems the intensely patriarchal values – which she has been subjected to – have presented her with and the pride she feels at being a Somali woman.

Conclusion

In this chapter I have reviewed what a life histories or oral histories approach entails. I have considered the value it brings to this kind of research which seeks to really get to the bottom of why so many women from diverse backgrounds continue to feel marginalised and vulnerable to oppression and gender-based violence of differing forms. I also explored how the researchers themselves felt about using this approach and what they felt they learnt as a result. The researchers agreed that they found the approach had almost therapeutic qualities which they experienced positively, giving them the opportunity to learn more about themselves and in some cases discover things about their own histories previously blank. However, for many it was also painful unearthing emotions they thought they had buried or that they did not realise were lurking beneath. Each researcher could have left this process at any point but none did; they felt the outcome was worth the risk and should therefore be recognised for the courage they have shown. Ebyan summed up the difficulties not just personally, but also the agonising over representing the lives of others sensitively and accurately. I then ended by emphasising again that these stories, far from essentialising women's lives through a focus on culture, actually bring out many overlapping issues. Women's lives are complex and so too are the problems that they encounter. Secularism has in many instances made the problems women face worse, both because it acts as a barrier to understanding the experiences of different women and because this lack of knowledge pushes BME women further into the margins of society, isolating them from support networks. What the stories also show is that culture, religion and tradition remain defining features of women's identity and that the secular context of their wider lives makes little difference to traditional practices. For the women who heard and recorded these stories the process has been empowering in ways unexpected but rewarding.

2

Somali Memories of Female Genital Mutilation

Isha Abulkadir

Introduction

This chapter contains oral histories from two Somali women who recount their experiences of female genital mutilation (FGM). As is detailed later, using the term FGM is highly contentious but enables a clear political statement to be conveyed about its brutality. In this chapter the traditional term 'circumcision' is also used as this is how it is often referred to by Somali men and women. The women whose experiences are told here are first generation migrants, one a young newly married woman, the second a married mother of two children. This chapter in part reflects on why women continue both in the UK and Somlia to put their daughters through this practice, which I vividly remember as a horrifically painful experience. Clearly, as the stories and responses documented here attest, patriarchal beliefs and values maintain circumcision as a fundamental rite of passage for many girls both in the UK and Somalia.

In trying to understand why this practice continues, the categories of 'culture' and religion' are critically examined. I included, in my research, some reflections on FGM from two imams based at a mosque in south London predominantly attended by Somali Muslims. Their reflections highlight the internal tensions within the Somali community in the UK as to the continued need for FGM. These imams do not support the practice and argue that there are no religious teachings to support it. The views captured here reveal the interesting way in which people use the categories of 'religion' and 'culture' differently to explain why this practice continues. In other words an artificial separation between the spheres of 'religion' and 'culture' emerges as a way of enabling those who oppose the practice to preserve the purity and authority of their religion by claiming FGM to be 'cultural'. In a similar way those who support the practice believe it is sanctioned by and through religious doctrines, rules and codes of conduct surrounding appropriate female behaviour. As discussed in the Introduction, the relationship between religion and culture is endlessly complex. Religious and cultural values and beliefs are highly fluid and constantly shifting. Religious authority is aligned with notions of divine truth that cannot be questioned. It therefore follows that any practices which can be endorsed by religious teachings cement themselves as an accepted/normal part of everyday life. Culture is often seen as the more problematic area of life. Sources of cultural authority and wisdom are less fixed, more dependent on knowledge passed down through generations. Cultural knowledge is endorsed by leaders, whose own standing as sources of authority may be periodically questioned. It appears easier to challenge what goes on in the name of culture because no ultimate divine truth is being questioned.

The people whose stories are recorded here employ culture and religion to help express their attitudes towards female circumcision. Whilst the persistence of FGM is fundamentally due to patriarchy, the fact that religion and culture are part of how different Somalis understand it means they must form part of the analytical frame through which it is unpacked.

This chapter is divided into three sections: the first reviews some of the research previously conducted on the prevalence on FGM both in the UK and parts of Africa, specifically the so called horn of Africa where it is most prevalent. The review identifies two main foci of the literature: firstly the medical implications of the practice; and secondly, the legislative attempts to eradicate it. A third area of literature comprises an anthropological approach which attempts to give a nuanced and complex picture of how FGM forms part of a wider gender ideology. This ideology endorses the strict control of women's bodies; FGM is presented as a way of maintaining a societal and patriarchal status quo. The second section presents the life histories of two women who have experienced FGM; one of these stories is mine.

I deliberated about hiding my identity, but for me, the motivation behind writing this chapter is to highlight the brutality of FGM. I don't want to hide behind a false name; I want to see my story in print in the hope that it might help me create a platform upon which I can challenge this practice. The last section analyses these narratives and searches for answers as to why such an obviously barbaric practice continues. In seeking explanations this section draws on the analytical continuum outlined at the start of the volume and in the first chapter, which draws attention to the variety of interlocking factors shaping an individual's outlook on life and attitudes towards FGM.

Context and analysis of FGM

There are four ways in which female genital mutilation ('FGM') takes place: (i) by cutting away the clitoral hood with or without the removal of the clitoris; (ii) by removal of the clitoris with partial or total removal of the vaginal lips; (iii) by removal of the clitoris, vaginal lips and stitching of the vaginal opening or (iv) by involving tribal mutilation or burning of the vaginal orifice using corrosives to narrow the vaginal passage. The most extreme form of female genital mutilation is the excision of the clitoris, labia minora and labia majora followed by the sewing together of the raw edges of the vulva so that only a small hole remains through which urine and menstrual fluid may pass. (Ramage, 2009: 1)

As stated in the Introduction to this chapter, research on female genital mutilation (FGM) or female genital cutting (FGC) predominantly focuses on the health implications of the practice and/or the legislative framework developed to try and eradicate it. The Genital Mutilation Act 2003 makes it a criminal offence which carries a penalty of fourteen years' imprisonment on indictment and conviction. The 2003 Act extends the provision made in the 1985 Prohibition of Female Circumcision Act to include any offence of FGM which takes place outside the UK on a national or resident of the UK.

Despite this legislation, according to Toubia (1994) FGM is practised today in twenty-six African countries, with prevalence rates ranging from 5 per cent to 99 per cent. It is rarely practised in Asia. It is estimated that at least 100 million women are circumcised globally. The practice is known across socio-economic classes and among different ethnic and cultural groups, including Christians, Muslims, Jews and followers of indigenous African religions. Toubia writes that:

> ... from the perspective of public health, female circumcision is much more damaging than male circumcision. The mildest form, clitoridectomy, is anatomically equivalent to amputation of the penis. Under the conditions in which most procedures take place, female circumcision constitutes a health hazard with short- and long-term physical complications and psychological effects. The influx of refugees and immigrants from different parts of Africa to North America, Europe, and Australia in the past decade requires that physicians and other health professionals familiarise themselves with the practice and its ramifications for their patients. (1994: 56)

In the UK the Department of Health in 2007 funded a study to establish the prevalence of FGM in this country (see Dorkenoo and Morison, 2007). This study sought to estimate the number of women and girls in England and Wales living with FGM and those under fifteen years of age who are at risk. This survey revealed that about 30,000 girls in the UK are deemed to be at risk from this practice. Of the 303,454 migrants to the UK from countries in which FGM is practised, the study estimated that in 2001 66,000 women had undergone FGM. In Somalia 75 per cent of women are thought to have undergone this procedure. According to Sen and Kelly (2009), 'while this provides some baseline data the absence of a community based survey means that the impact of Government and civil society efforts to eradicate FGM in the UK are yet to be measured' (2009: 33).

Sen and Kelly also point out that women with FGM only become known at the time of pregnancy and childbirth mainly due to the significant complications the practice can cause during this period. The actual picture of the prevalence of FGM in the UK is therefore hard to discern.

Since the practice tends to emerge during a woman's pregnancy it is the medical profession in the UK who have been at the forefront of responding to the implications the practice presents. This also accounts for the large amount of literature and research directed at understanding the medical impact FGM has on women in the UK. In 2009 Ramage, Strauss and McEwen conducted research to explore the care received in the UK by circumcised Somali women. The key findings of this study revealed mismanagement in the care of circumcised women during pregnancy and labour which exacerbated their physically vulnerable condition during this time. Many Somali women experience acute problems during pregnancy and labour. Ramage, Strauss and McEwen found the communication between medical professionals and Somali women to be poor. Many Somali women reported that they felt their midwives held stereotyped and negative attitudes towards them, viewing them as 'backward' because they had been circumcised. The existing pressures migration brings in the form of language barriers, racial prejudice and lack of confidence and knowledge on how to interact with state services were compounded by these experiences of childbirth in the UK. Practical suggestions emerging from this important report stressed the need for midwives to possess the necessary clinical knowledge and skills to deal with women who have been circumcised. A second recommendation stressed the need for greater urgency in raising the possible complications with women during early pregnancy.

Better care of Somali women during pregnancy begins with better communication. Sensitive and responsive communication has to be founded on cultural understanding and an appreciation that each woman has her own story to tell of FGM. Listening to these stories is a vital step in building trust and challenging the stereotypes that surround the lives of Somali women in the UK. The stories told in this chapter offer a glimpse into the differing responses and views women themselves hold of the practice but also reveal the lack of engagement in this issue by secular state agencies. Sen and Kelly (2009) also highlight this inadequate provision of services specifically tailored to respond to the needs of women who have undergone FGM.

As Dirie (1991) points out, contrasting points of view can be identified in the attitudes towards female circumcision; for example, while it increases women's value in Somali eyes, it often degrades them in the eyes of the outside world. According to research conducted by

Morison, Dirir, Elmi, Warsame and Dirir (2004), 'Living in Britain from a younger age appears to be associated with abandonment of female circumcision and with changes in the underlying beliefs on sexuality, marriage and religion that underpin it. Groups identified with more traditional views towards female circumcision include males, older generations, new arrivals and those who show few signs of social assimilation' (2004: 1). This publication offers an optimistic outlook that FGM is fading as generations living in the UK are extended. The research presented in this chapter suggests that any assumptions that time will see this practice eradicated without the need for the state to act are misplaced.

There is much less contemporary anthropological literature on FGM than that written from a medical or legal perspective. A volume by Gruenbaum (2001) presents the different interpretations of FGM that often contradict and operate to distort our perceptions not just of a complex understating of the practice itself but of the women who endure it. She writes:

> To the Western eye, there is something jarringly incongruous, even shocking, about the image of a six-year-old girl being held down by loving relatives so that her genitals can be cut. Yet two million girls experience this each year. Most Westerners, upon learning of the practice of female circumcision, have responded with outrage; those committed to improving the status of women have gone beyond outrage to action by creating various programs for 'eradicating' the practice. But few understand the real life complexities families face in deciding whether to follow the traditional practices or to take the risk of change.

Gruenbaum goes on to point out that Western outrage and efforts to stop genital mutilation often provoke a strong backlash from people in the countries where the practice is common. She looks at the validity of Western arguments against the practice. In doing so, she explores both outsider and insider perspectives on female circumcision, concentrating particularly on the complex attitudes of the individuals and groups who practice it and on indigenous efforts to end it. Gruenbaum finds that the criticisms of outsiders are frequently simplistic and fail to appreciate the diversity of cultural contexts, the complex meanings, and the conflicting responses to change. Drawing on over five years of fieldwork in Sudan, where the most severe forms of genital surgery are common, Gruenbaum shows that the practices of female circumcision are deeply embedded in Sudanese cultural traditions and underpinned by religious, moral and aesthetic values, and in ideas about class, ethnicity and gender. Her research illuminates both the resistance to and the acceptance of change. She shows that change is occurring as the result of economic and social developments, the influences of Islamic activists, the work of Sudanese health educators and the efforts of educated African women. That does not mean that there is no role for outsiders, Gruenbaum asserts, and she offers suggestions for those who wish to help facilitate change. However, any intervention must work within the wider cultural and religious environment rather than challenge from the outset the entire way of life of which FGM is one part.

The 'custom question' has been explored by Mustafa Abusharaf (2006), who writes that 'generations of supporters of these contested practices espouse a wide range of ideas about why female circumcision constitutes an important part of their cosmology and world-view. These practices, which others often contemplate with horror and trepidation, are exalted and sanctified through the very language used to refer to them. Most of the local terms translate as ritual purification' (2006: 2). The language used to describe this practice is highly politicised. I, as my story reveals, have very personal reasons for using the term 'genital mutilation'. As Abusharaf (2006) states: 'the term circumcision is used because it translates directly into African languages and because researchers have found that using FGM alienates those who still support the practice and must be persuaded to relinquish it'. A third term has emerged – genital cutting – which is hoped to be less politicised, offering a literal description of what happens in this practice. However, beyond the diversity of terminology the question remains: is female circumcision a virtuous act of purity and rectitude? Two opposing views emerge and dominate contemporary debates, one authorising cultural accommodation and the other advocating the observance of universal human rights. The former view has been widely vilified for sanctioning violence under the guise of culture and the latter has been reproved for its ethnocentric stance towards cultural rights.

The life histories approach taken in this volume allows those affected to project their views on how the practice should be viewed and responded to by the outside world. The views are far from unanimous, which reflects the extent to which circumcision is an integral part of how many Somali women understand their world and place in it. I hope that as new opportunities are realised by women in my community they may begin to reflect and reorientate their world-view in a way that preserves our distinct heritage but rejects the suffering it brings to women.

Reflections and memories of FGM from Somali women and religious leaders

The tone of this chapter now shifts to one that allows the reader (I hope) to gain a more personal glimpse into the life experiences of two circumcised Somali women. Included in this section are the views of two imams based in south London. Both women whose stories are told here are deeply religious; Islamic teachings shape their approach to life and represent a fundamental part of how they identify themselves. It is therefore useful to look at the extent to which in London religious leaders sanction or challenge FGM.

Story 1: Ishmahan

Ishmahan is a lady that I have gotten to know and over time we have built a friendship and mutual respect. She was happy to share with me her experiences of being circumcised. Ishmahan is a mother of four and she is still married to the father of her children. The night that I was interviewing Ishmahan both her husband and daughter were there. At first Ishmahan was really shy and unable to open up to me despite the fact that we are friends; this indicates the extent to which circumcision, understandably, is such a private experience. After a few questions she started to open up and talk about the her experiences. I told her I knew this was difficult but it was important that we as Somali women talked about our experiences, challenged assumptions and were heard. The interview was conducted in Somali. I have transcribed the conversation below, including the questions I posed to her.

So now Ishmahan, at what age did you get circumcised?

When I had been circumcised I was the age of seven years. I was injected before the procedure so therefore I could not feel the pain but I did feel the pain of the injection.

Were your parents there when you got circumcised?

Yes, both of my parents were there and so were all my relatives; they were the ones that had said I should get circumcised, including my grandmother.

Were they happy – I mean your parents and other relatives?

Most defiantly they were. When my parents told my other family relatives, they all came to visit the night before the procedure and stayed with us until I was brought home from the doctors. Also they had agreed with my parents and they said that it was important for me to have the procedures take place.

Were you circumcised by a doctor; I mean by a real doctor?

Yeah, I was circumcised by a real doctor; first he injected me and then he started the procedures. As I said, I did not feel anything.

How long did the procedure take?

The procedure did not take that long; it was about thirty to forty-five minutes long. I did not feel the pain until the anesthetic went off: that is when I felt the pain and it was so painful, it made me cry.

Was your doctor female or male?

I was circumcised by a male doctor. After I had been taken back home, my legs were tight together for at least seven days, and during the day I had to sit and sleep on the floor.

Going to the toilet was really hard as well, because every time I went to go to the toilet it hurt and burned. After the operation it took three days for me to go to the toilet. I was really scared of the pain.

When the family could not make me go to the toilet, they had to call the doctor to come and make me feel scared, so then I could go to the toilet.

When he came, he said to me that he was going to do the operation again and I was still feeling scared. On the fourth day I managed to go for a wee.

How did you feel about the operation and sitting home all by yourself?

The only feeling I had was the pain. I was so jealous that all my friends were outside playing while I was at home doing nothing, sitting on the floor every day for seven days a week. I could not do anything as I was not allowed out for seven days.

If you could not walk, who did things for you?

Well, what I did every day was sit on the floor and do nothing. Everything was done for me, from getting changed into my clothes to giving me a wash every day. Every morning one of the female family members would give me a strip wash and change me into my day clothes. They would do that again in the evening.

So what happened after the seven days?

After the seven days, the doctor came to check if it is getting better, that is, dry, and also if the stitches can come off. He checked if I was getting better and said everything was okay, so now he could take the stitches out.

After the seven days were you allowed to go outside and play with your friends?

Yes, after the seven days I was allowed to go outside and play with my friends, but I had to be cautious, because it had only been seven days since I had the operation. I had to protect myself so I would not get torn apart or hurt myself again.

How long after the operation did you feel yourself again?

After the seven days, it took at least three weeks more for me to feel confident and happy not to protect myself and not be cautious every time I was playing with my friends.

As a child you do not know the difference until you reach teenage years, because that is when you become a woman and also that is when a girl gets her period. When I reached my adolescent years and when my periods began, every month the first three days of the period would be really painful; it reached the point where I cried myself in bed for those three days, unable to get out of bed. Taking painkillers did not help at all.

Do you think the pain that you were going through every month had something to do with the circumcision?

Although people say the pain was due to the circumcision, I did not make the connection. I just thought that the pain was part of the period and so it was normal. But my aunty did say to me that I was experiencing the pain because of the circumcision.

Also, a day before my period was due I had abdominal pain. I also used to and still bleed a lot. When the pain got worse I myself blamed the circumcision for the pain that I was in.

What age did you get married?

I was twenty-three years of age when I got married, and this is the first time that I had been with a man. This was also the first time that I had intercourse. Having intercourse was really painful the first seven days

As a girl that had been circumcised there are two pains that you would face once you get married or have intercourse. The first pain would be the one where your virginity would be broken and the other pain would be the one where your clitoris had to be opened up, because the circumcision makes your clitoris so small that nothing can go in.

I felt the pain of the intercourse until I was pregnant with my first. I think this may have had something to do with circumcision because you just do not feel pain every time you have intercourse.

After the honeymoon I got pregnant with our first baby, and nine months later I was ready to give birth. By the time I was taken to the hospital I was open 2 cm. I had to be taken to the hospital, because the pain was getting worse and worse. Until the next day I was unable to bear the pain and the doctors said I was not ready to give birth. A few hours later the doctors said that since this is the first baby and that I was in a lot pain they would keep me in the hospital to make sure that both me and the baby were okay.

Whilst in hospital I was unable to sit or sleep, so I spent the whole night standing up. During that night the doctor told us that I would have the baby by 8 o'clock the next morning. But when 8 o'clock came I was still in pain and this time the doctors could feel the baby's head. However, I did not have enough energy to push the baby. The doctors told me that the baby did not have enough fluid and so they said the baby was in danger and that they will have to do c-section operation. That is how I had my first baby.

Do you think the circumcision had something to do with you suffering with the birthing of your baby?

Yes, and that is what the doctors also blamed, as did my husband.

What about the birthing of the rest of the children? I mean, how did that go?

I can tell you for sure that I did not suffer as much as I suffered the first time around. With my second child it only took four hours of pain and birthing. It was different for each child and I would say the first baby was the worst. When I was giving birth to the third child, I was overdue so the doctors had told me to come into hospital so that they could induce me and they said that they would inject me so that the pain would come quickly. They also broke my waters.

So what is your opinion on female circumcision?

My opinion on female genital mutilation is that it is a clean procedure if it is carried out the right way. If it is safe from infection and other disease, I would say it is something that will help every girl on this planet.

How could you say that female genital mutilation is safe, since the procedure has many effects on the individual?

I am not saying the procedure will not have any effect on the individual. I had certain problems that I had to face, but I did not think it was due to the circumcision and it also did not stop me carrying on with my life.

What about the pain that you and other ladies have experienced from your husband due to this dreadful procedure?

I mean sex was painful and there was no pleasure every time, as the whole point of the procedure is to cut off the pleasure for the girl, so that she does not go around wanting to sleep with any guy.

Would you make your daughters go through the procedure?

Yes I would, but only if it is simpler than the one that I went through, and also if they would not feel the pain that I had endured after the operation. I would try and do things differently and easy.

Do you think the government of this country should allow circumcision?

Yeah, I think they should allow circumcision and they should allow each individual to circumcise their children.

Even if the government allowed circumcision, does not the religion forbid circumcision?

The religion says that you should not make someone bleed or have someone's blood on your hand. However, if the doctors cut only a small part, then it would not be painful and the individual would not lose so much blood.

Whilst doing this interview with Ishmahan, her husband was also there and he interjected saying, 'You ladies, all you care about is the pain that you go through. What about the husbands?' I asked him about the husband's experience; he replied, 'Don't you know as well as the ladies going through the pain, us guys have a difficult time dealing with the pain that our wives go through. I mean, when someone is saying to you that she is in pain it's real hard. You cannot have intercourse with someone who is in pain.'

Is female circumcision allowed in Islam?

After hearing and documenting Ishaman's experiences I wanted to understand why she remained adamant that her daughters should be circumcised. I wanted to explore the extent to which religious leaders, given their influence in the Somali diaspora, support this practice. Below is an interview conducted by a male colleague, also Somali; direct access to male religious leadership as a Somali woman is rare. I gave my colleague the list of questions I wished him to explore with the imams and his interviews are directly transcribed.

Imam 1: There is disagreement whether it is allowed or not, but the prophet said Muslim people are not allowed to have someone else's blood on their hand. Cutting someone and making them bleed is having someone's blood on your hand, and that is the same as you killing someone.

Imam 2: Female circumcision is not allowed in the Islamic religion, as you are hurting someone, and furthermore you have someone's blood on your hand.

Some people are saying that you're allowed to cut a small piece of the clitoris. Is that allowed?

Imam 1: Well, I am not sure, but if you are doing that then you should make sure that the person does not bleed.

Imam 2: As far as I am concerned you should not hurt someone; you should not have someone's blood on your hand, as the prophet forbade for someone to have someone else's blood on their hand.

As imams of mosques people respect you. Shouldn't you do something about female circumcision?

Imam 1: Well, we try our best, but female circumcision is not about people following the religion, it's more about people following and doing what their ancestors used to do. So therefore you cannot really change someone's view, as they will always mix religion with culture.

Imam 2: People confuse religion with culture. Female circumcision is not a religious thing – its a cultural thing. As much as we want to change people's view on circumcision they are not educated enough on the effects that circumcision has on the individual. Because if people were educated then parents would not harm their children.

Also, if they follow their religion, they would not have someone's blood on their hand. Even if they are your children you still have someone's blood on your hand.

The imams do not talk about the roles of men and women, and their arguments that it is against Islam because it risks a person's blood being spilt highlights the extent to which they are not linking this practice to wider and more deeper rooted gender inequalities. They talk about it being wrong because it involves hurting the woman, but do not address the reasons why it happens. The continuing presence of FGM as a rite of passage for Somali girls is clearly sustained by cultural beliefs and values around female honour. FGM is the first step in a girl's journey into womanhood, encompassing marriage and children. Marriage and traditional gendered ideals around female conformity to a specific model of heterosexual marriage is clearly at the heart of the ideology that sustains this practice. Female circumcision has been placed under close scrutiny and condemned by activists across the globe. As such it is often talked about in isolation from the process of marriage that begins for a woman in her childhood. Somali leaders have had to find a response to it, a reason why it continues even when its barbarity is clear. The interviews with the imams highlight how they both separate religion from the sphere of culture which enables them in turn to distance themselves from FGM. However, their explanations also reveal the extent to which they remain supportive of the wider patriarchal and gendered ideology that underlies it. In other words, whilst they condemn FGM mainly on the grounds that blood is spilt, which is strictly prohibited in Islam, they hold firm to traditional gendered ideas of the roles and responsibilities of men and women. As research on FGM in Africa reveals, it is this strictly upheld patriarchal environment that has allowed FGM to flourish for so long because it insists on women's subservience to men through marriage. FGM is one mechanism through which women's conformity to married life is assured.

Now I turn to my story ...

I was eight years old when I got circumcised. I lived with my grand-mother from the age of three to eleven years of age. My parents got divorced when I was the age of six years old; after that, my grandmother was responsible for both me and my brother. So back then whatever my grandmother said went; we had no choice but to obey her without question. So it was my grandma that said I would be circumcised; she told me I would be getting circumcised about two weeks before the day.

As a child you don't really know anything about circumcision. Being a child you would think circumcision is basically playing with your little friends outside the house. These are the thoughts that went through my head when she told me. Of course the experience is very different and I was not prepared. If I had been, I would have tried to find some way of struggling even then as a young child.

The night before the circumcision both of my parents came to the rural area where I lived with my grandmother. That night was the most special night as I had all of my friends, my family and also family friends. Older men came to our house so they could read the Quran to me and and they wished me luck. I felt very special and cared for at this moment at least.

While everyone was having fun, I and three other girls were taken to anther house, which belonged to the parents of one of the girls who was getting circumcised with me. I slept that night thinking what was going to happen to me early the next morning, knowing something was about to happen but not knowing what. Early the next morning we were all woken up to have a shower and eat breakfast, ready to be taken to a lady's house. We did not know then but she would be the one to carry out our circumcisions.

I vividly remember during that early morning how I was given a shower and breakfast, but that I could not eat breakfast. Although I had little real awareness of what was about to happen, somehow inside I knew it was not going to be good and well, basically, you cannot really eat anything when someone is going to be cutting part of your body.

Even the other girls could not eat their breakfast. The elder ladies with us just ignored our fear and did nothing to try and ease the tension which must have been obvious to them. We were all feeling so scared at the prospect of being taken to the lady's house. We lived in a rural area of Somalia, so there was no transport to take us there, so we had to walk. It felt like a long walk, and I remember the fear building with every step. We did not speak to each other.

When we reached the lady's house, my legs started shaking, taking slow steps as I entered the house. As I got more inside I could hear her talking to other ladies. We were urged into the lady's room to say hello to her. As we went in I started sweating and shaking at the same time.

We each said said hello to her. She responded by asking us if we needed the toilet and that if we did we should go now because – and I remember her words – 'as soon as we start the procedure you will not be able to go to the toilet – so go now'. I was terrified and I decided to take this chance for time on my own and went to the bathroom. I stood in the bathroom thinking about what was going to happen to me as soon as I got on that bed. I began thinking that I was not going to be scared; I told myself not to be frightened, to be strong. I said to the ladies that I would go first, so that I didn't have to wait and be more scared watching the others. I knew I could not escape and wanted it over with.

So I came out of the bathroom and I was told to take my trousers off and lie on something that looked like a bed, but was not a real bed. Standing around the bed there were already five ladies waiting for me, I did not know at the time but one would carry out the operation and the other ones were there to hold my hands and legs, so that I wouldn't kick about.

As I lay on the bed two of the ladies held my legs and the two others gripped my hands. As the lady started to do what she simply regarded as her job, another lady came and said something to her. I don't remember what she said or even if I heard but I do remember that following their exchange I started to scream louder as the pain increased. I also remember that no one was listening to my screams, no one seemed to care about the pain I was suffering. The team of ladies just let me cry throughout the operation while they talked; I remember them talking endlessly throughout it all. A few minutes later I could hear the main lady saying, 'She is bleeding. I need something to stop the blood.' The others gave her a sponge to stop the blood and she pressed down hard with it.

After that, I was taken home by one of the ladies, still very upset and in great pain. When I was brought home I saw my mum, and other family members were there sitting and waiting for me. The lady that carried me put me on the floor and for the next few weeks that is where I stayed from dawn till dusk.

In rural areas the practices of and around circumcision differ compared to those carried out in the city. For example, I was not allowed to eat my normal diet; instead I was made to eat corn-made porridge every morning. I was not allowed to eat pasta or rice and sweets; I actually don't really know why I was not allowed to eat those foods but I remember that being denied my usual diet just made the whole experience even worse. In the city such dietary restrictions are not practised.

In the area in which we lived there was no doctor or any kind of Western medical care so I had no painkillers and had to endure the pain for weeks. I ask you to imagine being an eight-year-old child having to feel the pain of someone cutting a part of you and being offered nothing to help take it away, no good food or comfortable bed and especially no pain relief.

Adults and children were coming to visit me and some would play with me for a while, but no child wanted to stay inside the house for long – they all preferred to be outside in space and the fresh air. I felt lonely, with very little to take my mind off what had happened to me, which I did not understand because no one had explained it to me, not even my grandmother. All I knew was that for some reason it had to happen. Many thoughts went through my head. Was this a punishment? Had I done something wrong? These thoughts just increased with the pain and loneliness.

Every time I wanted to go to the toilet I could not pass urine because I was so scared of the pain. The first day, Mum kept taking me to the toilet but every time I said I wanted to go, once I got there I simply could not go. At one point I remember she got really angry at me and said, 'Don't you know that you are heavy. I cannot pick you up and take you to the toilet and you don't do anything.' It felt as if no one understood what I was going through. It was miserable.

So the next day when I still could not pass urine my family threatened to call the lady and make her do the procedure again. This made me really scared and I started wetting myself. Although this was terrifying, at least I was able to go to the toilet.

My physical recovery was slow and quite difficult. It took at least a month and a half whereas the other girls that had been circumcised with me took much less time and even came to visit me after a week. I am not sure why it took me so long but I remember wishing I could have healed as quickly as they.

For a week I had the sponge stuck on me. My family could not remove the sponge as it was stuck with dried blood. Someone from outside had to come to take the sponge off me and it was painful as they ripped some of my skin off at the same time. This meant some of the healing skin was removed, leaving a raw wound again. I think perhaps this is what took me so long to get better. After a week I was allowed to walk around the house, but I was not allowed to go outside and play with my friends.

When I asked both my grandma and my aunties why I couldn't go outside to play with my friends, they replied, 'Your body is raw and it's only been a week since the operation, so you may still hurt yourself.' I remember I was upset and annoyed by the fact that I could not go outside and play with my friends.

Although there were no biomedical treatments available for the pain or to help the wound heal, there were traditional remedies and practices. Every evening for the two weeks following my circumcision, before bed my grandma and my aunties made a hole in the ground into which they put wood which they then lit. I then sat over the lit fire while it was still not too hot for a few minutes. This process was repeated every evening because it was believed that the smoke of the fire would cure me, ease my pain and prevent infection in much the same way as antibiotics. I did in fact feel this treatment had some effect and to a certain extent numbed the rawness of my genital area, making it feel better, but it took time and these positive effects were not felt straight away.

After a month I felt better and so was finally allowed to go outside and play with my friends, although I was told to be careful. As a child my main preoccupation throughout this ordeal was to get better and start playing with my friends again – this was my main concern. I had no real understanding of the long-term impact of what had happened to me and only a little insight into why circumcision was practised. This naivety about the impact of circumcision continued even as I grew older into my teenage years before my cycle began. I had no awareness of the lasting physical and mental impact of what I now refer to as 'female genital mutilation'. As soon as I began to menstruate, slowly I realised that I would live with the consequences forever. My periods were really painful month after month, and no painkiller had any effect. I even tried to use stronger painkillers and it did not help. By the time my periods started I was in the UK and I went to see my GP who said that the pain was due to my circumcision. He prescribed some tablets which he claimed would make me feel better, but they did not work for me; the pain continued.

That pain stays with me even today, a lasting reminder of what I suffered. I got married at the age of twenty-two, a happy occasion which I looked forward to. Although I have not become a mum yet, and have therefore not faced pregnancy and childbirth, which I know my circumcised body will find difficult, I have found sexual intercourse a bit difficult. This is not a surprise as it is well known that anyone who has been circumcised will find sexual intercourse difficult. The physical reason is because I faced two problems: one is the normal pain women feel when they first have intercourse and then there is a second level of pain as the clitoris is closed by circumcision and must be opened by your husband. If I was able to give advice to someone who had been circumcised, I would tell them to go and get it opened so it is easier for you to have sexual intercourse with your husband. I strongly believe that people need to be educated on the long-term effects of circumcision, both physical and emotional. This is what has motivated me to write up my own story as part of this chapter. I don't think parents really appreciate the implications of circumcision for their daughters' lives, especially in the UK. Even though my grandmother was circumcised herself it was as if she had forgotten the pain and trauma it must have caused her or somehow justified the need to put me through it. As with the case of Ishmahan, some women seem to be able to block out or dismiss the pain and still claim it is an important practice even though many imams condemn it as against Islam. I have tried to understand this viewpoint, this insistence that it is an important part of what it is to be a Somalian woman. In my attempt to get answers, one day I rang my grandmother and asked her without anger why she put me through this practice. She said 'it is about honour; a girl who is not circumcised cannot prove her honour in the future, it will make it difficult for her to get married'. She also talked about identity and linked circumcision to what it is to be Somali women: 'to suffer the pain of circumcision makes you stronger, an important trait for Somali women'. She also said 'I went through it, it is what we do.'

I have strong views that female genital mutilation should be stopped, because it does not bring anything useful to a girl's life apart from pain and stress. I have always had this view. Living in the UK has not influenced the way I see this practice. I have always from the day it happened to me known it was wrong and somewhere even at eight years old made the decision to challenge it and to stop it happening to my sisters and to others around me.

Conclusion

These narratives reveal the extent to which women disagree over the necessity for FGM. The first woman seems inclined to think she should get her daughter circumcised even though her own recollections of the practice are harrowing. She sees circumcision as an important part of becoming a respectable married Somali woman. Her husband is reported as being forthright in condemning the practice and does not want to see his daughter go through it. Whatever his reasoning, which seems to be primarily rooted in a concern that his own sexual pleasure is compromised, he may well be more assertive in preventing his daughter from going through a similarly painful experience. In my experience, I claim that it is primarily women who are responsible for putting their daughters through circumcision and cites many conversations in which husbands have been vocal in condemning it. I would be wary in suggesting that this undocumented evidence says anything clear about women's culpability in their own oppression or rather the complex and ambiguous relationships Somali women have with FGM. What it does suggest is that circumcision remains a highly contested issue within Somali culture and that migration has done relatively little to resolve this. I am angry and saddened by my experiences of FGM and fear for my future because of it. I think that circumcision continues in the UK because women are scared that if they don't put their daughters through it they will not be able to get married. In other words, patriarchal pressures continue to impact on how women think about their own bodies despite living in a secular state that supposedly has a legislative framework designed to support and protect them.

3
Tales of Somali Marriage in the UK

Ebyan Ahmed

Introduction

This chapter contains three narratives woven together and offering differing perspectives on Somali culture told through a focus on marriage practices in both Somalia and the UK. In the first section I offer reflections on my culture and throughout this chapter description is interspersed with a personal narrative. By taking this approach I hope to reveal something of how I and many other Somali women negotiate a path between cultural heritage and the secular society of the UK. I lived in Somalia for only a brief part of my early childhood before leaving for the UK. I moved to the UK because my country broke up into civil war. My family had to leave behind not only our home but also many relatives and friends to come to a place where our lives would not be in danger. Nobody wants to leave their home for a foreign land, but my parents took that courageous step so that we could have a future, so that we could live. As a result I know my parents worry that their children will lose their heritage. I hope in this chapter I allay at least some of those fears, but I also want to explore how my generation has responded to life in the UK.

The passage below reflects what I hold as the essence of my heritage and I try to paint a vivid picture of a land and culture steeped in history and vibrancy because I am very proud of my roots. I find it upsetting that too often the image of Somali women portrayed in the press is that of a downtrodden circumcised women, victims of a harsh and brutal culture. Whilst I am strongly against circumcision and have successfully managed to escape it, I am worried that this is all people think of when they meet a Somali woman for the first time. My cultural identify is founded on so much more than this one practice. Weddings are an important way of celebrating all that is good and positive about my culture, hence the focus of this chapter.

Somalia is known as the horn of Africa; our nation is full poets, lecturers and scholars. I hope the stories in this chapter will enable outsiders to explore my culture through descriptions of how we participate in and celebrate weddings, the food, clothes and customs. Weddings are important events in the UK because they connect us with the essence of what it is to be Somali. Weddings for Somali women are important: we each dream of what it will feel like to get married and hope it will bring us lasting happiness. Growing up we are told stories by older female relatives about how exciting our wedding day will be and the happiness it will bring our parents to know we are now secure in marriage. Growing up I remember talking with my female friends about what dress we might wear, the venue and most of all the food. In this chapter I share my reflections as an unmarried woman thinking forward to marriage alongside stories told by Somali women of their weddings. These stories also offer glimpses into married life and reveal its harshness and the demands and expectations placed on women after marriage that we are not told much about as young girls. Patriarchy clearly structures the relationship between husband and wife but of course this is not the picture given to us in our childhood nor is it a situation unique to Somali women.

Importance of weddings for Somali women in the UK

Interestingly ethnographic research conducted by Guerin, Hussein and Guerin (2006) into Somali weddings in New Zealand suggests that the celebrations around marriage bring women important and positive psychological benefits. The researchers argue that women's participation in these events was contributing positively to their mental health and well-being, helping to generate feelings of belonging in their new country.

The activities that the women engaged in before, during and after these parties were highly social, involving many women in the community. If some women could not attend or contribute to one thing or another, there was always something else in which they could be involved. For example, if a woman could not actually attend the wedding party, she may still help prepare food for the party. Having a number of activities over sometimes even a few weeks afforded women in the community multiple opportunities to socialise with others in the community. Guerin, Hussein and Guerin (2006) also witnessed repeatedly the women discussing current issues in the community, people's problems and solutions, and other issues of relevance to mental health while involved in this event.

What we are saying here is that it was not just the party, wedding, or the event *in itself* that was the important contributor to the well-being of many women in this community, but all of the social aspects of every activity along the way (2006: 4).

These findings certainly resonate with my experiences of weddings; they are opportunities for us to celebrate and immerse ourselves in our past and our heritage. However, conversations between generations during such celebrations also reveal changes in how my younger generation views our lives. Clearly the expectations most of us Somali women now have for our lives are different from those of our mothers and grandmothers. The extent to which these changes in attitudes will impact on marriage practices is unknown but it is likely that my peers will not tolerate the same kinds of strictly controlled lives our mothers have endured. What little research there is on changing patterns of marriage among Somali disapora groups certainly supports the view that women's expectations and life choices are shifting. Berns McGown (1999) compares the experiences of Somali Muslims in Toronto and London and concludes that in both contexts the divorce rates have increased compared with those in Somalia. Explanations are founded on the increased autonomy of women which is perceived as a challenge to male authority. Men in many instances are not the main provider which is traditionally the patriarchal norm; this produces tensions between couples that in a significant number of instances leads to divorce (see also Chapter 4 where similar shifts are identified in the Zimbabwean diaspora community resulting in tension and in extreme domestic violence). This suggests that migration has to some extent impacted on traditional gender identities, but as the stories in this chapter attest, patriarchy still dominates women's lives and represents the obstacle they must navigate around if they do not wish to entirely conform to what tradition dictates. Marriage practices are embraced and preserved by all generations, the celebrations surrounding them offering us the chance to feel positive about our Somali heritage – but they also give time for sharing and exchanging views on life and the future.

Reflections and insights of marriage

I begin by retelling a conversation I held with a close friend of mind, also Somali; it began with me asking:

How did you meet your husband?

Well actually it is a funny story; he is my uncle's nephew (my auntie's husband). One night he came to my auntie's house; he was looking for my uncle. I was with my friend. My friend liked him – she was saying he was handsome; I agreed with her that he was attractive. She couldn't stop talking about it. She gave me a headache, was going on and on and on … all day and night. I told her I could get her his number if she wanted but she didn't want it – because she is a Somalian girl. Somali girls believe it's too embarrassing for women to get a man's number and call. So she left it at that.

A year later, he was still single. He was ill, so my uncle brought him round so we could take care of him. I was staying with my auntie at the time. He noticed me, when I was bringing him some food, and he told my uncle that he liked me, and that he was ready for marriage. My uncle told my auntie and my auntie asked what I thought. I told her, yes, I'm ready for marriage. I thought he was very handsome. Strange how things came about. He was round twice ill in this house.

One day he texted me. That's how I knew he was a wussy. He was a mystery man. (Laughs to herself.) He texted me the lyrics of an English song, I think by Coldplay: 'I saw your face in a crowded place.' At that time I used to listen to music but I was not that familiar with it because it is not my type of music. I tried to figure out what he was trying to say because he didn't tell me who he was. A day later I realised that those were lyrics. But I still thought that was such a nice thing to do.

That night he called and told me who he was. I remembered him. He said he wanted to take me out and I said okay But it didn't happened straight away. We kept in contact for a couple of weeks but I still didn't see him but he kept on saying he would take me out. Then we saw each other.

My marriage was sort of an arranged marriage because he asked my auntie out of respect. We saw each other a couple of times. We went out for about three to four weeks before the process of getting married happened. Then he arranged a meeting with my brothers to see and get to know them. He told them of his intentions to marry me because they are the ones who are responsible for me (my *mahram*). My father was alive (may Allah have mercy on him) but he was not in this country.

We then talked about setting a date. We agreed to have it in September so that my uncle from Canada could be here. All together, from first meeting each other to getting married was roughly a year. I found things were moving too quickly but it had to be done before my uncle flew back.

Marriage preparation and ceremony

The preparation took less than a week buying ingredients for the dishes. Because it was a small event, it was done in my auntie's house instead of a hall. The plan was that I could have a big wedding after a couple of months. On the day, loads of men came to the house (at least 200 men). Then the *mahir* (Islamic wedding ceremony) took place. Two groups of men have to be present and this is very important in order for the ceremony to take place. One group of men represented the groom, the other group the bride. There are no restrictions on the number of men in each party. For the groom they can either be made up of individuals who are blood-related, friends or tribal.

The representation of the bride is made up of males who are close blood relatives (*mahram*), in this case her brothers, while members of the same clan also have to be there. Unlike the groom, the bride is not present. The tribe members are seen as bringing honour and respect. The presence of male relatives at the ceremony is symbolic, showing that our family know who we are marrying into and so they will be watching out for us even after marriage. Symbolically the male elders are understood to represent a bridge between the bride and groom. If the married couple encounter problems they can turn to the elders to help them sort them out.

The two parties of men sit facing each other. Prior to the ceremony the groom's and the bride's families discuss who is going to bring the *sheik* (a man who has intensive knowledge on the religion of Islam).

At the wedding ceremony the sheik sits down facing the two parties representing the groom and bride and asks them do you (name) take (name) to be your wife. The groom replies 'yes'.

He'll then ask the same question to the bride's side and the party responds on the bride's behalf. I remember in the morning my brother called me to make sure I still wanted to get married and everything was still okay. I said 'yes'.

The groom then gives money to the bride's family; it is seen as rude and embarrassing if they take the money, so the bride's family then distribute the money among the guests. Distribution begins with the oldest and ends with the youngest. This particular ritual has no symbolic meaning beyond showing that the groom is a generous and nice person. In the UK the groom is expected to give a minimum of £500, but this is largely dependent on what he can afford.

Women and men cannot be together in the same room for religious reasons. A Somali wedding is usually broken up into two separate parts. First you have the *nikkah* or Islamic marriage ceremony which is attended only by men. After the ceremony vast amounts of food are eaten and the men generally socialise for hours on end.

In the evening a ceremony takes place for women in the main wedding venue which is elaborately decorated. During the evening event there is much dancing, so a big space is needed. Invitations are given by word of mouth and everyone must be included: if people discover they have been left out this will be considered hugely insulting. Furthermore it is considered embarrassing if a bride invites you directly to her wedding, so instead invitations are given out by her family members.

Before the bride enters the venue a ceremony known as *Baramburh* takes place. This is when all the elderly women get together, drums are brought out and a trance-like rhythm is played. The bride's and groom's names are mentioned and also those of their parents. Heroic stories are told of the bravery of the grandparents and great-grandparents. The tribes are praised and tales of their success shared. Every time high praise is given two women at a time jump into a circle that has been created for them by the crowd. The dancing turns into a competition in which the women strive to be the best. Mesmerising dresses are worn which are full of vibrant colours and hand stitched patterns.

The *Baramburh* can go on for a couple of hours or even more. Then a signal is given that the bride has arrived. We line up in our rows, starting from the door, welcoming her with smiles, claps and cheers. She walks up to the stage where a chair that is fit for a queen awaits her. She is wearing African dress (*hidio dakan*) that incorporates the colours of the Somalian flag. Cameras start to flash as everyone tries to preserve the moment. Music of the bride's choice is played in the background and a chant is started, *arasokadha wayyaah wahlo arwahiy* ('this is your wedding day ...'). Pictures are taken of the bride and her family. The bride takes her first dance with her bridesmaid, and close family members and friends, then the dance floor is open to all.

After an hour of greeting and dancing, people are seated for dinner. The traditional Somali wedding food is rice, meat – either lamb or beef – with vegetables on the side, a small portion of salad, and separately red spicy sauce with a sort of salty pita bread. Guests are given a variety of juices and fizzy drinks, no alcohol of course. Once people have been fed they have a quiet time and the bride will have a change of clothes. The bride will usually change into three different outfits throughout the evening. The music and dancing continues until sunset when traditionally the groom comes and picks up the bride from the venue to take her away from her family into her new home. This may be the only time that the groom comes in, but in this day and age as more women are getting married in the UK they have come to change that concept in that the bride and groom enter the event together. The groom brings his friends and it becomes a mixed party. This move towards mixed wedding parties is one of the biggest changes as it has traditionally been considered unIslamic for men and women to mix in this way. At the end of the evening everyone is given a gift basket containing sweets, drinks and cakes. It is seen as rude not to give guests something and even if you are poor you cannot let your guests leave empty-handed.

In Somali culture, the bride and groom are not meant to leave the household for seven days and seven nights so that they can spend some quality time together, to get to know one another and feel comfortable. Neither of the parties must cook or work; food must be brought to them as they are not allowed to leave the house. We have a party for the bride after seven days to welcome her into womanhood. This is when she gets presents, usually household gifts to help her create her new home. The elder women and those that are married will give her *saash* (material to cover the hair); these are woven with certain patterns and made of silk to represent that she is married. Those that are not married cannot part take in this ritual unless they are doing it on behalf of another married woman who could not be there, and when she goes up to give her the *saash* she must state the name and surname of the woman on whose behalf she is there. More drums are beaten and again the tribes are praised, songs are sung, dances are danced and food is eaten until the bride is given away to her husband for the last time.

Reflections after the ceremony
When I realised I was married, I thought to myself, 'What have I done?' It was a bit scary. I realised I was married now. I didn't regret it but I was excited and scared at the same time.

I didn't have a wedding; I wanted to do it but we decided not to because my husband wasn't happy about it. Because of the *deen* (religion) he had an issue with coming into a room full of women.

In Islam it not good for people to hear a women's voice, and marriage is the only time where it is permitted for a woman to shout in praise and happiness. She is allowed three screams. Marriage is an important factor in Islam. It is said that when you marry, it completes half of your *deen*. The reason for this is that marriage allows you to stay away from certain temptations of wrongdoings with the opposite sex. It also gives you responsibilities of taking care of your own family and so on.

Married life now

What is married life like now? What was it like to begin with?

It was very, very strange. You need to get to know each other: the way you do things and he does things are different so we have to adjust to each other. You need to let him know where you are and where you're going and what time you'll be back. I am still finding it difficult. Those types of things used to irritate me; in fact, they still irritate me even after four years. Before, I used to get up, get dressed and go and now I need to tell someone where I am going. Although I think my marriage is different we didn't really adjust to each other. He kept on doing his thing and I kept on doing mine.

At first it was hard to live with him (for the first couple of months). I used to argue and stress too much. First it was the wedding because at first he wanted it, then he changed his mind. But I wanted one, and we used to argue about that a lot. Then he told me he felt uncomfortable, and after that I let it go. I think not having a big wedding was the only right thing I have done in my life.

One thing that upsets me about him is his smoking, especially in the house. I told him about my dislike of it. He didn't listen. He took it the wrong way. Like I was saying the house was mine. That's how I know the guy was dodgy. He thought I was making some kind of protest against him, questioning his authority. He never stopped smoking. It was sort of blackmail – after a while I couldn't say anything because he made me feel guilty about asking about it. He only stopped when I got pregnant after two years. He is a typical Somali man.

A typical Somali man is a man who is the head of household. Although there is nothing wrong with that, the male views the female as not of much importance. I find that amusing because that is being small-minded. He thinks the woman should stay in the kitchen, cook and clean and serve him, that husbands should be seen as our masters when they come home. This is the way they see it and how they talk about themselves to us. My husband does not think I have an opinion or that I have a right to one.

I work and that was the biggest problem of all for my husband. He knew when we got married that I worked and that I intended to continue, but he thought that I would leave my job when we got married, straight away in fact. He thought I would leave and stay at home; I was never going to do that and he was told that. I think he thought he would be able to make me change my mind once he was my husband and had authority over me.

After recording my friend's story, I asked an older woman of my mother's generation to share her views about marriage and divorce with me. I thought that her opinions might offer insight into how the values surrounding marriage may or may not be changing in the UK. I found it much harder to get this woman to talk to me and so approached our conversations through a series of questions.

How are Somali marriages different in Somalia compared to the UK?

Tradition – people don't have clear separate roles. Women are too fussy; they want to go out all the time. They don't argue about who gets to work.

Do you think people run to divorce too easily?

In this country there's nobody that helps them, that keeps them together. If someone wanted to get divorced in Somalia, the elders would be called from both sides of the family – so that a compromise is set by both parties to the problem that they are having. Women go to the elder women in the family to ask for advice and guidance.

Why do you think people are getting divorced so much now? Would it be different in Somalia?

People don't have patience; you get a lot of help from your neighbours, friends and family. You have everyone to help. Here, everyone tells you to deal with it. The environment helps you back at home; here there are no Somali people were I live. I have no Somalis that live in my area, or are part of this community.

Can you identify key characteristics of a Somali man?

Somali men don't give flowers or presents; they are not romantic in any way. This action is not significant and they do not see it as a big deal. I don't really care. Young people might care, but I want him to be a nice person but flowers are not a big deal. I don't want something that dries up and dies in two days. I would rather have jewellery and gold. A man would buy a women presents when it was significant, such as when she's had a baby, or when she finds out she's pregnant.

When a woman gets married, she's his woman. She has her role, in the sense that she has to take care of him and take care of everything in the house. He works and provides for her and his family. It is his responsibility to bring in money as well doing weekly shopping for the house. Women should not carry heavy stuff or do laborious work. It is a man's job. There is no real reason for her to leave the house apart from to go see her family and on occasion go out with her friends. We go to weddings as well as shop. We invite our friends round to our house and socialise. We take good care of our guests, feed them with three-course meals, entertain them with wedding videos. This is the time to get to know what is going round town, the latest gossip. A woman has no financial responsibility as she does not work. When she wants money her husband gives it to her. In our religion it is in our *deen* that a man has to provide for a woman and give her everything she wants.

How do you feel about this?

It is his responsibility to take care of me so I don't feel bad about it. I am happy with having no financial independence, I don't have to worry about money. Here, men and women are on each other's tails. They both leave the house in the early hours of the morning, they leave their children with a babysitter. In Somalia there is no government that will help with that. Family is always on hand.

What are the different roles that men and women have played in Somali culture?

The man is the head of the house. He controls everything, and the wife obeys him. She is the one that looks after the kids. The woman is the carer of the household and the nurturer of the children.

The reflections of unmarried Somali women

I return now to my own reflections as an unmarried woman hearing this and many similar stories about married life from Somali women in the UK. I found it incredibly hard to conduct research on the lives of those that I love and care about. I felt as if I was delving into their lives, exposing them as weak, rendering them vulnerable to the readers of this book who might form negative opinions about them. I was worried that my informants did not really understand where their stories were going to end up, in other words in print to be read by strangers who had no connection to them but who would read and judge, perhaps harshly. It is one thing to share these stories in private where honest opinions feel safer to offer, but exposing yourself to the world is something else. Most readers won't know or understand our culture; they may not understand why we do certain things, or behave in certain ways. They are unlikely to appreciate the different values and traditions embedded into our world-view through our upbringing, none of which changes that much just because we are in the UK and not in Somalia – they shape who we are. However, because we have what seems like a different set of rules, others outside who do not understand can at times see our tradition as a threat to British secular society.

I don't want to misrepresent my family, friends and community and I thought about not partaking in this. However, after some consideration I reflected that using this approach, asking people to give their life stories directly, is the best way of conveying a balanced picture of life as a married Somali woman in the UK. I know my mother and friends are happy: they balance the patriarchal expectations of their husbands with their own aspirations and the opportunities offered to them in the UK. This book is not meant to slander in any way our people, our culture or our heritage. It is for people to simply understand that we have a different way of life and to provide a platform for at least a few women to describe how they experience it in their own words.

Reflecting on my own life as I move into the period when marriage becomes an actual possibility rather than something imaginary and talked about in childhood, I have mixed feelings about following the footsteps of my mother and friend into a marriage with a Somali man. Although of course there is no homogenous category of Somali men – they are all different – there are certain patriarchal expectations that they all seem to project onto their wives. This irritates me and I am worried how I will be able to fulfil my personal dreams within a traditional Somali marriage.

My main concern is the lack of sharing of domestic duties. I have not known any Somali man take an active role in the upbringing of his children with his wife. I accept that a mother is seen as the more important person in her children's lives from birth onwards; she carries them for nine months and then is the primary nurturer. Somali men see their role as the provider of the household, the head of the family. They definitely have the mentality that 'real work' is carried on outside the home in the real world, and women don't do anything at home but cook, clean the house for a bit and then generally put their feet up for the rest of the day. In other words, there is no knowledge or appreciation of what running a home and raising children actually entails. I am not sure I could tolerate this level of disengagement from my husband. I am not sure I would want to lead such a separated life from him either.

From what I have seen in my own family and heard those around me say, husbands expect a lot from their wives. They expect the house clean when they get home and their food ready at the table waiting for them.

To this day my father expects my mother, sisters and I to serve him like waitresses. He claims it is insulting to him to have to go into the kitchen; he should not be expected to get his own food and certainly not have anything to do with preparing it. As time has gone on he has eased a little in his gender views but only in so far as he permits his sons to also serve him; he does not stop them from helping a little in domestic work. This is a shift in his views; five years ago he would not have let them anywhere near the kitchen, making it clear to them that anything inside the house was women's work. I remember he would say to them if they began to do anything vaguely domestic, 'That is not the job of a man; one of the girls has to do it.' His views only changed when we started school and there were no girls left during the day to serve him, and Mum was tied up with the babies, so he turned to the boys to fill in. He obviously felt that it was better someone served him so he could avoid having to do women's work.

When it comes to cleaning, my father's patriarchal attitudes are even more strongly expressed. On a daily basis, as the babies grew up, my father would walk past their toys strewn over the floor avoiding ever having to pick them up. He had strong opinions about cleanliness and frequently would scold us for messing the house up. He would instruct us to clear up around him while he sat and watched. He views himself as superior – I still find this funny – and believes it is beneath him to bend down and pick up a simple toy from the floor. His view is not only that he is a man and so it is not his role to clear up but also that he has had children and they should take a role in looking after him and the home. Although I do believe that children should help around the house, what makes me so angry is when I am told to pick things up, cook and clean because I am a woman. I ask myself so often: what makes my brother less able to do domestic chores? My father is unshakable in his belief that women and men have different roles to carry out. A woman's place is in the home and man is the breadwinner. These roles are rigid and should not be altered or swapped between the husband and wife. Throughout my childhood my father would tell me, 'You do this because you are a woman.' Something inside me always reacted strongly each time I heard him say this to me, but I knew there was no point in challenging him – his views are far too rigid. I can see that this strict patriarchal way of organising and dividing roles and responsibilities has helped to create a stable family life which Somalis are proud of, because it has been accepted by men and women as the norm for so long. This clear distinction between the roles of men and women also seems to keep marriages together: both parties understand what they must do on a day-to-day basis and appreciate that in conforming to their roles they will be able to create and sustain a strong and secure upbringing for their family.

Although my own experiences growing up are not as extreme as this woman's I feel confused. For my parents, everything is so straightforward: they remain committed to continuing with the way of life they were brought up in back in Somalia. However, for my generation, much of our upbringing has been shaped by the wider society in the UK. I have conflicting feelings about my upbringing and the expectations, specifically around gender, that my culture places on me. I am proud of my heritage but at the same time I don't want to submit to the role of a housewife. I do want to get married and have children but I don't want to be told that this is my sole role in life. I want to feel I have chosen to do it. I want to challenge and eradicate the commonly held views that I have to have children because I am a woman. I also though feel pressured by the feminists who push women to reject domestic life in pursuit of a career. I don't know if I want this either but I already feel guilty at the thought of not having a job. Living in the UK has given me many opportunities but it has also brought difficulties into my life. I often feel as if I am stuck between 'a rock and a hard place'.

Conclusion

In this chapter I have presented insights into married life for some Somali women living in the UK. I began by presenting marriage as an important and exciting moment in a Somali woman's life. I explored the opportunities marriage celebrations present for women, moments to embrace and feel positive about our heritage but also times to share experiences and stories both good and bad. I then, through the presentation of two life stories, brought you into the day-to-day realities of life as a married Somali woman attempting to navigate between her heritage and the patriarchal expectations it brings and the opportunities available in the UK. There is nothing unique about the extent to which concepts of male dominance pervade family life in

Somali culture – indeed, wider British society is still inherently patriarchal – but what I tried to do in this chapter is emphasise the rigid gender constructs Somali women have to deal with. I ended by sharing my reflections on my upbringing, the anger and frustrations I experienced at my father's unfair assumptions that I must conform to a domestic role just because I am a woman. At the same time I feel guilty at the idea of not pursuing a career.

I have not yet decided the path of my life. I am fighting what feels like competing sets of expectations: my tradition and the feminist values I have come to embrace. The struggles I express here are common among my female peers in the Somali community: this is what we discuss and often make different decisions about. I hope more than anything that this chapter highlights the determination of many Somali women to change aspects of their tradition, specifically patriarchal structures. Changes are being forced from inside by women questioning the status quo and challenging the assumptions that their path through life is pre-determined. I feel optimistic, but also ask others to support us in bringing about these changes ourselves and in our own time.

4

Domestic Violence in Zimbabwe and the UK Diaspora

Esline Dzumbunu

After the economic hardships of the 1990s and the political and social unrest of the past decade many Zimbabweans left their homes in search of what they deemed 'greener pastures'. Zimbabweans migrated mainly to the UK, USA or South Africa. Like many Zimbabweans, l realised that l could not stay in a country that no longer offered me any future. My job in the bank was not enough to support me and my siblings in a decent lifestyle. Most of my friends who had gone abroad were constantly telling me how good London was and how l could easily get a job and save some money. My expectations were raised that after five or so years l would then be able to return home and buy a house and with the experience of working in the UK get a better job. In July of 1998, l packed my bag and l came to London, sad to leave my family and friends, but also full of determination. I had thought that in five years maximum l would be on my way home. Seriously, l thought London was paved with gold and l would just pick what l needed and go back home to set up my businesses. I know l was crazy to think like that, but the London you read about in magazines and novels is very different to the reality.

Over the years the only information publically available about the Zimbabwean communities in the UK centered on immigration, mainly the problem with the number of asylum seekers. The image projected felt homogenous; we were all lumped together and considered a problem, coming to the UK mainly illegally to scrounge off the state. As a result very little understanding was ever expressed about why so many Zimbabweans were coming to the UK seeking refuge. Little time was given in the media or literature to understanding the problems we brought with us and then continued to experience once here. Although gradually research is emerging that explores the experiences many of us face, some more difficult issues are left untouched. In this chapter I am going to explore an issue that has affected my life – domestic violence.

Before I begin I would like to acknowledge the fact that domestic violence, or violence against women at the hands of their partners or spouses, is not exclusive to our community. It is common in most communities and cultures. Its history for us is much more than a man's desire to gain control over his wife – many more issues are at play. For me it is very personal as I lost out on a relationship with my father and also being a family. It's for these reasons and more that I have decided to tell the stories of two women who have suffered at the hands of men (their husbands) who had promised to love and care for them. I am going to tell the story of my mother and a friend who were victims of domestic violence in Zimbabwe and in the UK. I was surprised to see that despite the generation gaps the nature of the violence was the same for my mother some twenty-five years ago and for my friend in the UK in 2007. Their stories, although different, bring home to me the extent to which domestic violence continues to blight the lives of Zimbabwean women even, ironically, after they move to the UK to escape violence.

Although I only present two stories in this chapter, they represent many similar narratives I have heard members of my diaspora community tell me over the years. I have no doubt that domestic violence represents one of the biggest problems facing Zimbabwean women in the UK, yet there is very little research exploring its extent, and few resources ploughed into addressing it. This chapter begins by reviewing the limited research conducted on domestic violence in Zimbabwe among the diaspora in the UK. It analyses the explanations given by researchers who seek to find reasons as to why it prevails so extensively. The chapter then presents the two life stories of my mother and friend before ending with my reflections on life as a Zimbabwean in the UK.

Reviewing the research

According to research conducted by Pasura (2008) the Zimbabwean population in Britain increased from 47,158 in 2001, according to census statistics, to an estimated 200,000 in 2008. Pasura (2006) conducted a mapping exercise of the geographical spread of Zimbabweans in Britain, showing that they are dispersed across the nation, notably in London, Birmingham, Manchester, Liverpool, Luton, Slough, Coventry, Edinburgh, Leicester, Sheffield, Doncaster, Bournemouth, Oxford and Bristol. The dispersal of asylum seekers to areas outside London and the south-east as part of the1999 Immigration and Asylum Act may have contributed to the dispersion. However, people also moved out of London to smaller cities in search of work and to follow social and family networks. The successful settlement of migrants in destination countries depends, among other things, on how they integrate into the labour market. The majority of Zimbabweans in the UK are highly educated professionals, belonging to middle- and upper-class families in the homeland (Pasura, 2006; Bloch, 2005; Mbiba, 2005; McGregor, 2007). McGregor (2008) described Zimbabweans in the country as living and working in sharply polarised circumstances:

> On the one hand, there are those who have secured professional work or set up their own businesses, as well as those who have secured refugee status ... they have a degree of basic stability derived from their rights to residence/work and their incomes, and are in a position to plan careers, mortgages ... At the other extreme, there are those trapped in unskilled jobs with insecure legal status, many of whom struggle to meet their own basic needs and family obligations and live in fear of deportation. (McGregor, 2008: 466)

Pasura argues that for Zimbabweans in Britain immigration status can be understood as a creating class divides, as it shapes the opportunity structures for migrants as well as determining their everyday lives. The majority of Zimbabweans in the country maintain regular and sustained transnational ties with the homeland by engaging in diaspora politics, keeping kinship ties, sending remittances and in their involvement with diaspora associations. Although the classical conception of diaspora underscores homogeneity, the Zimbabwean diaspora in Britain is fractured and fragmented.

Literature specifically exploring instances of domestic violence in Zimbabwe is limited. According to Stewart (1992), activists in Zimbabwe from the late 1980s worked hard to resource and create a number of shelters for women suffering from domestic violence. Much of the early writing on this topic was written by activists rather than academics. Schneider (2000) argues that out of this literature emerged different theories as to the reasons for such prevalent levels of domestic violence which include a rights-based approach, feminist and cultural explanations. Theories as to why domestic violence occurs are of course vital if successful responses are to be put in place, a link emerging between explanation and solution. Stewart argues that a multi-causal approach is needed in order to understand the complexity of domestic violence in any context, and the Zimbabwean one is not different. She also warns against simply transposing a Western response to domestic violence onto the African context. She says this is particularly evident in the formation and application of the rights-based discourse. The rights discourses are founded on an individualistic perspective whereas African thought is often more relational. Women in Zimbabwe are caught within a web of complex connections. African societies, so Stewart goes on, are not founded on individualism, but rather concepts of the family are given priority. A woman's reproductive capacity is vital to the stability of the family and is owned by her husband. The rights discourse, now articulated globally through conventions, declarations and conferences, stresses the need for the individual woman to challenge the violence she suffers which conflicts with this most relational way of approaching life and requires some women to reorientate the way they approach the world.

Feminist explanations of violence in Africa focus on the pervasive gender inequality: 'almost every traditional African society was patriarchal and a woman's place within this scheme decidedly subordinate. Institutionalisation of this inequality remains common in African customary law, women have no right to inherit from their husbands, are excluded from ownership of land and are almost without remedy upon divorce' (Stewart, 1992: 852).

Gender inequality is widespread and domestic violence often treated as a sub-section of this. African feminist writers such as Ofei-Aboagye writing about domestic violence in Ghana attributes it largely to the subordinate position, passivity and economic dependence of many women in her society. So the struggle to end domestic violence is often seen as part of a broader struggle to rectify gender equality. In Zimbabwe, Armstrong carried out a study of domestic violence which involved interviewing twenty-five male abusers and seventy-five female victims of spousal abuse in the Shona-speaking region. Her findings suggest that violence most frequently arises out of quarrels over money and jealousy. For example, violent arguments erupt when the wife simply asks her husband for money. This is seen by the husband as a challenge to his authority as the head of the household, which includes control over the family's finances. Similar violence often erupts when a wife asks her husband where he has been, suspecting he may be having an affair. In challenging his fidelity the wife is also questioning the husband's right to pursue other relationships. Whilst female sexuality is strictly controlled, men are free to pursue other relationships, increasing the risk of HIV/Aids transmission and potentially draining the family's finances, especially if the husband accepts responsibility for additional wives and girlfriends. Armstrong's research identifies the most commonly reported causes of arguments which escalate into violence: disputes about the husband's traditional economic obligations; the husband's anger over a wife's perceived failings to adequately fulfil the role of a wife within the traditional division of household labour; and husbands becoming violent if they feel their wives are not being sufficiently submissive to their authority. The research as a whole suggests that domestic violence is used as a mechanism to ensure women conform to the patriarchal model of womanhood.

Contemporary literature exploring the experience of the Zimbabwean diaspora in the UK includes the volume edited by McGregor and Primorac (2010), and whilst it covers and records experiences of exclusion, relationships with home, health and employment difficulties as well as the continued campaigning for freedom and peace in Zimbabwe, the issue of domestic violence does not emerge. Pasura (2006) analyses the performative and lived realities of the Zimbabwean diaspora in Britain. The research explores the way in which both public and private spaces of the diaspora are important arenas in the construction and reconstruction of gendered identities. It is based on multi-sited ethnography, comprising thirty-three in-depth interviews and participant observation in four research sites. The findings suggest that the challenges to patriarchal traditions in the hostland in terms of women's primary migrant status and financial autonomy, the different labour market experiences of men and women, and egalitarian laws have caused tensions and conflict within diaspora households. Although Pasura does not present clear evidence to suggest that these shifts in gender norms have led to an increase in domestic violence, as already stated there are no official statistics that enable us to measure the extent of domestic violence among this community. However, Pasura's research is useful in helping us understand why domestic violence is likely to continue as a serious problem for many Zimbabwean women in the UK. The research reviewed above on the cause of domestic violence in Zimbabwe highlights that any perceived disruption to gender norms and specifically women's roles often causes an eruption of violence. Pasura highlights a shift in women's roles and opportunities in the UK which clearly undermines the patriarchal norm. Once in the UK many diaspora women pursue employment and therefore acquire a degree of financial independence in addition to or perhaps even in some cases instead of their domestic and reproductive role. It is possible that this shift causes tensions that are often expressed violently by men who see this independence as a threat to their authority.

Stories of domestic violence

My mother grew up in Harare's biggest township of Mbare. Her family had been one of the privileged few who had managed to secure houses in Harare as my grandfather had worked as a policeman. As their family grew bigger my grandfather was not able to pay the school fees in the urban schools for all eight children. That meant that the younger ones had to move to the village and go to school there. My mother says, 'I remember my mother walking five miles at 4 a.m. every morning to take my sisters to school, because they were scared to cross the mountain and the thick forest to get to the main road.'

My mother's story retold in her own words

Before the move to the village, I remember a time when my family was actually very happy, and even when we first moved to the village. My father used to come to the village every weekend and brought with him foodstuffs and sometimes even treats. The brothers and sisters loved the milky sweets my father would bring wrapped in brown paper. We looked forward to the weekends when we would eat meat and not the usual spinach and tomatoes. My family was considered to be one of the better ones as we didn't rely entirely on the land for our food and the fact that we had better tools and cattle that helped us in ploughing and tilling the land. My mother was a hard worker and spent most of her time in the fields, while we went to school. We specialised in growing maize, peanuts, sweet potatoes and sunflowers, and what we harvested in the first few years was sold to the markets in Harare or we would take with us when we went to school and try to sell at the main road to motorists from neighbouring towns and cities. We also took with us wild fruits. The money we got from the sale of our produce and wild fruits would go towards our school fees and sometimes we would buy bread and tea leaves.

My father after one of his weekend visits decided that he could no longer afford to pay my school fees and he decided that I was to go and live with him in the city and look for a job. I had mixed emotions as I really loved school, but I also wanted to give my younger siblings an opportunity to carry on with school. Reluctantly I agreed to go as I didn't want to be stuck in the village without school. That Sunday I packed my bag; I didn't have much so it wasn't a big bag. I was now dreaming of the stuff I was going to buy for myself and also for my siblings in the village. I made a promise to myself that they would eat meat, bread and butter every day.

Finding a job in Harare was harder than I had anticipated. I didn't have any qualifications and hadn't even finished high school. Living in the city was very difficult without a job, as was having to rely on my father for everything who also had to support my mother and my siblings in the village. That same year my father started to drink heavily and he was enjoying the lifestyle of single men in the cities. Every day after work he would pass through the 'beer halls', as they were commonly known in those days. These were places where men who worked in the industrial areas and factories would go to socialise and meet friends from other industries and factories and also meet women. Single women who didn't have work would go to the beer halls to meet men who would then give them money and pay for their accommodation as well. I remember a few Fridays waiting outside these beer halls for my father to give me some money to take to the village and for food and to pay the house bills in city. In those days the men that worked in the city were paid weekly on Friday and as a habit most of them would buy foodstuffs at the Mbare markets and then get on a bus to the village. This is what my father used to do before he was seduced by the city life and forgot his responsibilities in the village. My mother and siblings were left desperate as there was no more money coming to her and the children. They had to now rely totally on the crops they grew in their fields and the wild fruits they were selling at the roadsides.

My mother was now in a very desperate situation, and I remember how my father would treat her. The few times my father went to the village he wouldn't bother to buy any foodstuffs, but he would expect to eat like he was used to when he was in the city. If she didn't provide what he wanted, he would make so much noise and call her nasty names and sometimes he would even hit her. After this he would find an excuse to go back to the city. It was so painful to see my mother being treated like this, but we wouldn't do anything to help. One time I tried to challenge my father, with severe consequences. He was so angry that he threatened to send me back to the village and that week he didn't even leave any money for food. After that I didn't say anything as I really needed to stay in the city to continue looking for a job. I told myself that I would help my mother better if I had a job. Looking back, this was the first time I experienced the effects of domestic violence. I didn't realise the extent of the violence against my mother, as she did everything to cover my father's violence against her and his neglect of the family. It was later on that she talked openly about the violence she suffered at the hands of my father.

The violence against my mother intensified when my father became involved with a woman he had met at the beer hall. My father was so taken by this woman that he forgot totally about his other family; she moved in with us and took over everything in the house. She was now in charge of the food money, which had been my responsibility. She would cook, but wouldn't feed me or my brother or sister and she was nasty to us. When she had children, my father built her a proper two-bedroomed brick house with a kitchen and living room in the village, very close to my mother's mud hut. My father would visit her and not even go into my mother's hut or even speak to her. If my mother or my siblings tried to speak to him or his other family he would get very angry and blame my mother for the disturbance. This would even get violent.

Through all this my mother turned to God. She found a church which became a place of refugee and solitude for her and the children through the violence and neglect by her husband. She would walk ten miles every Sunday to go to church. I always questioned my mother about how she could do that, but I was to discover what my mother meant later on in my life. The priests would visit her in the village and would constantly offer words of support and even sometimes food and money.

While in the city and trying to look for a job I met John [pseudonym]. John was very good to me; I fell in love and I was convinced that I had found my husband. For a little while I was happy and this was a way out for me. John was working and making decent money even though he lived with his parents, but he had his own room and had a better life than some of the men in the township. Unfortunately this union wasn't to be as I fell pregnant and John was so angry and didn't want anything to do with it. He even went as far as to blame me for sleeping around. Hurt and pregnant I had no choice but to return to my mother in the village as my father didn't want to know and blamed me for not behaving. He even went as far as to say that it was my fault that I had got pregnant and that John wanted nothing to do with it.

Back in the village, I spent so many months crying about what could have been and wasn't going to be. I felt betrayed by the person who had claimed that he would marry me and take care of me. My mother, full of wisdom, sat me down and made me realise that I had to be strong for the baby I was carrying. Fari was born in February 1972, a beautiful bouncy baby girl. For two years I stayed in the village looking after my baby and also assisted my mother and younger siblings grow crops for our food and to sell to buy clothes and pay for school fees. By this time my father had stopped all contributions to my mother's household. According to him, he wasn't going to look after people who didn't like his wife and kids. He continued to come to visit his other wife and children, but didn't even bother to find out how we were doing, unless he wanted to scold us for something his precious family had reported.

When Fari was two, I decided that I needed to go back to the city and look for a job to support my family. It wasn't even enough for them to just sell their produce; they needed more money for food. The harvest from the previous year hadn't been good as the rains had been late and they hadn't had enough water for our livestock and vegetables in the gardens. My mother agreed to look after Fari, so I left and went back to stay at my father's house. I went round to all the people that l knew and asked for work. I realised that it wasn't going to be easy to find work but l was more determined this time to find a job, not only for myself but for my daughter as well.

One weekend in 1973 I was at church in the village when l met this man who took my breath away. I later discovered that his name was Alex, and that he was in the village visiting a relative. He came across so confident and he approached me and introduced himself. I was very excited and had butterflies in my stomach. I immediately liked him and was even picturing myself being his wife. We spent the afternoon together and he came to the house to see me. After I went back to the city he kept in touch with me, telling me his ambitions of running a three-star hotel. Alex constantly told me that he loved me and how he was going to marry me. Eventually l threw caution to the wind, packed my bags and went to stay with him in Bindura where he was working. Bindura is a town that is about forty miles from Harare where my mother was staying with her father. I didn't have anything to stay for as l still hadn't found a job. I had decided to stay with him and soon enough I was pregnant and Alex sent a message through his uncle in my village that he was intending to marry me. Soon enough we had a common law marriage. After we were married my husband found a job in a hotel in Gweru and we moved to the midlands. My mother decided to continue taking care of the baby so as to give me time to bond with my new husband, and also as I was expecting another baby.

We quickly settled in Gweru. My husband's job was going well and we were blessed with a baby girl in July 1974. My husband was very happy but looking back, that is the time I realised about his excessive drinking. He even got in a fight with my elder brother, who lived in the same township as us, after they had been drinking together for hours in the neighbourhood beer garden. After the fight, it was clear that we couldn't stay and also the drinking had begun to affect my husband's job. Before long he had found another job in Kariba, a tourist town with lots of hotels.

My husband was a very intelligent man; he had been able to go to school after he had been awarded a scholarship by an NGO who had also sponsored his management course. He was one of the few people in Zimbabwe who had been intelligent enough and spoke fluent English to be employed at the front of the house in a five-star hotel in the 1970s. In Kariba my husband was working for the Cutty Sark Hotel as its manager. He was very good at his job and won many awards. As my husband worked, I stayed at home and made sure he had a clean and homely place to come back to. He was earning good money so we could afford to buy some furniture and even a television. It was my duty to make sure that my husband would have a clean and tidy house to come back to. I was really proud of my home, but looking back it looks like that was the beginning of our problems. My husband would insist on dinner being ready for him when he came home and he insisted on the house being his way. At first I didn't mind this as I had my hands full with a toddler and all the housework and getting to know our neighbourhood.

After we had our second child, my husband began to change. He was drinking excessively, blaming it on the stress of work and looking after the family in the village as well. Every time he got drunk he would come home very late, sometimes in the early hours of the morning, and demand his food and he would expect it to be hot. If it wasn't he would make a lot of noise and I remember the first time he raised his hand to me. I had gone to church and came back later than normal, which meant that his food wasn't waiting for him when he came home. As soon as he came in I could tell he wasn't in a good mood. He started shouting and cursing because there was no food ready. I tried to explain but it seemed I made it worse. Without realising what was happening, I suddenly found myself on the floor with hot mealie porridge on my legs and my baby on my back. I cried out for my husband to help me take the baby off my back as she was now screaming from the pain after the fall. I don't know who called the ambulance, but I heard the siren and they came into the house and took me and the baby to the hospital. When I woke up in the hospital my husband was sitting next to the bed, looking very worried. He kept on apologising for his behaviour and how he never meant to harm me and how he didn't know what happened to him. We were discharged the next day and my husband had bought my favourite chocolate and had got my friend to cook our dinner. I forgave him as I could see that he was really sorry and I believed it could never happen again. How wrong was I? This was the just the beginning. My husband went from just scolding me to giving me a slap or even two whenever he didn't like something I did. He kept on telling me how stupid I was and how I should be like other women who knew how to handle and take care of their men.

The beating got worse over the next year and I was actually relieved when he was on the night shift, because it meant he was not going to drink and then come home and hit me. One time he came home during the day and saw me talking to my neighbour's husband; he was so angry that he didn't talk to me or the children. He accused me of sleeping with the neighbour and the pastor from our church. He started shouting, and he grabbed me by my hair while punching me with the other hand. It went on for what seemed like forever. He left me lying on the floor and he went out without even looking back at me. My head was ringing and my lip was swollen and bleeding and my whole body was sore. Eventually I got up and walked to the clinic for some treatment. As usual I gave them a story of me falling off a stool in the house while trying to change a bulb. I'm sure they didn't believe me but they respected my privacy.

Like my mother, I then found myself finding comfort and friendship in the church. I would go there when I needed someone to talk to or when I needed refuge after the regular beatings. Now I understood why my mother had braved the long distance to and from church as I found myself being totally dependent on the church and the pastors for moral support and sometimes a place to hide.

Looking back, I can't explain why I stayed for so many years with such an abusive man, but where was I to go? I had three children, no qualifications or job experience, and also I was a married woman and my father would have just sent me back as in our culture a man had a right to discipline his wife and show that he was boss. I think I even believed that I wasn't a good wife as my husband would constantly tell me all the things I was getting wrong. I couldn't even tell my sisters all the abuse I was suffering as my husband always acted like a nice man to other people. I remember the few times my sisters visited me in Kariba. My husband was the perfect host, arranging a cruise, sightseeing and even a stay in his hotel for all of us. My sisters went away saying how lucky I was to have a husband who was so attentive and considerate. Unknown to them I was going to almost die after him hitting me because he had spent too much money on my sisters.

I really loved my husband, and I actually believed there was something wrong with him that made him so angry and need to hit me. It was only later that I realised that his work was suffering as well. His drinking had begun to affect his work; therefore he was taking out his frustrations on me.

I remember vividly the day I left my husband. For months he had been almost permanently angry and he was hitting me almost every day. This day he came home at around 2 a.m., drunk as usual, and asked for his food. I got up to warm up his food. I didn't realise that he had walked into our bedroom. My daughter was sleeping in the bed as she wasn't well. I had forgotten to take her back to her room when she fell asleep as my husband didn't like her being in our bed. He always used to say that that caused children to be spoilt. When my husband saw my daughter in our bed he got angry and started shouting and saying that I didn't respect him yet he was working hard and providing for us. By this time I had put his food on the table. He opened the basin and threw the *sadza* at me. It went straight for my eye and I fell back; immediately he was on top of me punching me and he tore my blouse and loosened the wrap I had used as a skirt. He left me with just my underwear. While on the floor I heard my daughter screaming as he had thrown her to the floor. I don't know how I did it, but I just grabbed my daughter and ran out of the door in my underwear. I kept running in between housing as I was afraid that he would follow us. As I continued to run holding my daughter I realised that I was never going to go back. It wasn't about my life alone – it was about my children's lives as well. He had never been violent or abusive to the children, but today he had changed. I realised that I wasn't going to risk my children's lives for my own fear. I prayed and prayed as I ran in the dark. As the first light broke, I was surprised to see how far I had run. I got onto the main road and saw a hotel. I went in and asked for some clothes and some food for my baby. They were so generous and they even gave me some money to get to my elder sister in Harare who was now married and working as a nurse.

I can't say that leaving my husband changed my life for the better, but it was a start. I started travelling the country selling clothes and foodstuffs from Botswana and South Africa. At first it was very hard, but I recognised that if I was to change my life and my children's lives I needed to be strong. With the help of my mother and my sisters I was slowly getting my life back and I didn't have that voice in my head constantly telling me how stupid or useless I was. I had taken back my life.

After my mother left my father, he lost his job after he got into trouble for having sex with an underage girl, but he managed to convince the judge so he was only sentenced to two years in prison. After serving the two years he found another job at Guruve Hotel, a new hotel a few miles from his village. My sister and I even visited him before it was opened. After only a few months he got into a fight with the owner of the hotel and he lost his job; he then found himself in the village with his new wife having to work in the fields for survival. He passed away in 2004 and I regret that I didn't get a chance to know him or even have a relationship with him.

Unlike my father, my mother blossomed after she left the abusive relationship. All her worries of how she was going to provide for her children were now at the back of her mind as she became an entrepreneur overnight. It led to the opening up of a shop and bottle store in Churumanzu where she met her husband. Her new husband took her to London and the violence she suffered is just a memory now. I should acknowledge that it wasn't easy for Mum to get back any confidence or self-esteem, but I can proudly say that my mother in her fifties, and with no formal qualifications, is in the first year of a BA (Hons) degree in Community Service and Enterprise.

Mary's story

Mary is a woman who found herself 'sleeping with the enemy'. She had a good job with the Harare City Council after being awarded a Business Administration degree by the University of Zimbabwe. Like every young person, she had a dream to work outside the country and earn more money and support her family. This is her story in her own words.

I was so excited to be starting my new job with the City Council and couldn't wait to see my office. I had taken a glimpse of it during the interview process, but I didn't remember the size or what was in it. I was hoping I would get a computer with an internet connection as I was looking forward to updating my Facebook and my emails. I hadn't had the chance or money to use the public places. I was even looking forward to the first pay: $300, that's what my contract had said. I wasn't sure how I was going to make it work, but it was better than nothing.

After a few months at work, I realised that I needed to find another job or apply to South Africa, like most of my friends from university. Before I could even start my applications I was introduced to a man who was on holiday from London. He was okay, not normally my type, but he looked like he was completely taken by me. For the next two weeks I saw him every day: for lunch, dinner and even road trips. He was very generous and I think I was actually in love with him.

After he went back to London, we talked every day and each time he would tell me how much he loved me and couldn't wait for me to join him in London. Looking back, it might have been more the excitement of leaving the job I hated and also the country that really influenced me. Six months after he left he sent his uncles to our house to ask my father for permission to marry me. My father wasn't happy since I had only known him for a few months, but all the other elders, including my mother and my aunties, were very happy that I had found a husband who would take me to London. You have to understand that London to the people in Zimbabwe was like heaven on earth and everyone thought that the minute you got to London you would have loads of money. I suppose their motivation was based on the life I would have once I got to London. One of our neighbour's children had gone to London, and now they had a bigger house and a couple of buses. Their life had changed so much with the help they were getting from abroad.

On the day of the traditional marriage, my mother made sure we had plenty of food and she even invited all of our relatives to be witnesses. Jack didn't disappoint; he paid a very good bride price and even paid my father's four cows and my mother's as well. My parents were so impressed as they had never seen anyone pay the full bride price and the cattle before and even my uncles and aunts were singing his praises. He was the perfect *mukuwasha* (son-in-law). During the marriage ceremony he had also asked for a church wedding, which my parents had agreed to as long as it was to be held in my village. Jack didn't have any problems with that, so my parents started preparing for the wedding day.

Our wedding day was on a beautiful sunny summer's day, exactly a year after I met Jack. He had refused my parent's help with the cost of the wedding, so he spent a lot of money to make our day perfect. I was the happiest person on earth that day as I felt so beautiful and I was marrying the man I loved and in a few weeks I would be moving to London. This was my dream coming true. After the ceremony Jack took me to South Africa for a week, before he flew home and made arrangements for my moving to London. I couldn't wait to join my husband in London; the days seemed to drag on and on.

Finally the wait was over. The day I got on the plane for London, I was so nervous, frightened and yet excited. I was going to be with my husband; surely I had no reason to worry. At Heathrow airport, Jack was waiting for me with flowers. He looked very happy to see me, but after we got into the car he looked distracted. His phone rang and after speaking for a while, he just hung up. He seemed angry and then he just opened the window and threw the phone out. I was so shocked by this and his sudden anger. I asked him what was going on, but he didn't answer. We drove in silence for about an hour and it looked like we were going away from London. I desperately wanted to ask him where we were going and what had made him so mad, but I couldn't bring myself to do that.

A few more minutes and Jack parked in front of a house I later on discovered was in Luton. After he parked, his mood seemed to change. 'Welcome home, my Love,' he said while helping me get out of the car. It was a lovely house, but I was surprised how small it was as he had told me stories of his three-bedroomed house, with a garden. I had pictured those big houses I had seen in Greendale back home with a swimming pool and enough space for a vegetable garden. The inside was decorated beautifully, clean and very tidy. I even thought to myself that I would need to maintain the standard. Once inside the house Jack went into a frenzy on the importance of keeping safe. He forbade me going into town by myself, or giving anyone our telephone numbers. He said that if the police saw me on the street, I would be deported or other people would be jealous of my being here with him and they would tell the Home Office and I would be deported. Without knowing it, these were the first steps in my isolation, leading to violence and abuse.

Two days after I got to Luton, I asked Jack if I could phone my parents and let them know that I had travelled well. He then said that I shouldn't worry as he had phoned the day I arrived. I could see that he was getting angry, so I didn't ask again. Jack's anger was such a shock to me as I hadn't seen this side of him in Zimbabwe when we had spent time together. It wasn't just the anger; it was also his obsessive behaviour. He wanted his food cooked in specific pots, and on his plate he didn't want his rice touching his chicken or his vegetables. He wanted the house cleaned three times a day and also I wasn't allowed to go outside, not even into the garden. From the day I got to Luton, I felt like a slave; the man I loved was not the same man who had picked me up from the airport. I was living with a stranger who was so angry with me and didn't have a kind word to say to me. He scolded me every time and to make sure I did what he wanted he decided to quit his job and stay at home so that he could keep an eye on me.

In the first two months after I got to Luton, Jack forced himself on me every day, claiming that he had bought me for a lot of money and that he could do what he wanted. He would call my parents names, and say how they loved money. I cried myself to sleep most nights after he fell asleep. I felt like the woman in *Sleeping with the Enemy*. I was in a foreign country where I didn't know anyone, with no means of communication. I didn't even know our address, and looking back, I don't remember seeing any post come to the house. Jack really made sure I was completely dependent on him and only him. For twelve months Jack kept me locked in the house. I didn't even go into the garden, with no communication with my parents or friends (we didn't even have a phone in the house). When he needed to go out he would lock all the doors and take the keys with him. I was his prisoner, but I didn't know what my crime was. This was the man who had claimed to love me, but treated me like his slave.

In my first twelve months with Jack, I almost died as I started to bleed and I was in terrible pain. I didn't know what childbirth was like, but I knew instantly that I was in labour. I called out for help, for what seemed like forever, until I heard someone breaking the window to the living room. Our neighbour had heard my cries and came to assist me. This could have been my way out of my situation as the police were called to find out why I had been locked in the house. Jack was first to answer; he told the police that I was new to England and didn't realise that I had locked myself in the house. I had no choice but to agree with him and I even apologised for wasting their time. I gave birth to a beautiful baby girl, but my husband was disappointed as he had wanted a boy. This was the first day he hit me and from this point it became a regular occurrence. Every time he didn't like his food or if the baby cried he would hit me.

The beating increased as our financial situation worsened. With the arrival of the baby, the little money he was getting from benefits was not enough for all of us. The baby needed more things we couldn't afford, but he was not prepared to go back to work or let me try to find work either. He kept saying that if I went to work, I would meet other men and I would leave him and how he would kill me if that ever happened.

The hardest thing over the eighteen months I stayed with Jack was the isolation. I didn't have anyone I could speak to or turn to. Our relationship of husband and wife was non-existent; we didn't even talk at all. He was always out and he would always lock all the doors. I couldn't see a way out of my situation. Before I came to the UK, I was an active member of my church in Harare and my faith was very important to me and I believed God was in total control of my life. When I met my husband I even believed it was the will of God, but now I feel like God has left me and I have lost my faith. I cannot even pray. I decided I wasn't going to believe in a God that wasn't there for me. My God wouldn't let me and my child suffer like this.

It was on 21 December 2008 – I remember the day like it was yesterday – when the baby woke up early, which upset Jack. He demanded that I attend to the baby so that he could continue to sleep as he was tired. I looked at the clock and it was 5.20 a.m., I got up half asleep and went into the baby's room. Before I could even pick up the baby, I heard Jack shouting, so I ran back to our bedroom. Jack was on the floor and it looked like he was having a heart attack. I went blank for a minute and then I dialled 999. The ambulance came and took him to hospital. After they left, I then realised that this could be my way out. I was concerned for him, but my desire to be as far away from him as possible was greater. I decided that there was no way I was going to be anyone's prisoner again. This was my chance to take control of my life. They say God works in mysterious ways; for me this was his way of releasing me from this prison that was my husband's house. I didn't stop to consider that I had nowhere to go or the fact that I didn't know anyone I could turn to for help. I quickly packed a bag with the baby's clothes and a few of mine. I found £100 in Jack's wallet and I left the house, almost running. I couldn't believe I was actually leaving.

I walked around the neighbourhood in circles for a long time, not knowing where to go. After three hours, I went into the police station and asked for help. They felt sorry for me and one of the officers took me to an abused women's shelter. I have lived in the shelter for about two years, but I have no regrets. Although I don't have the life I had dreamed of, my safety and that of my child is more important. With the help of the in-house counsellors, I got my confidence and self-esteem back. I even managed to find part-time work in a solicitor's office as an administrator as part of my therapy. There are many more challenges I have to overcome in the next few months, but I have my freedom and that's what's important to me at the moment and I am also working on forgiving Jack for what he did to me.

Conclusion

The stories presented here, despite the generational and contextual differences, are remarkably similar. The move from Zimbabwe to the UK did nothing to loosen the patriarchal expectations of Mary's husband. If anything, he became more fearful of losing control of her, regarding his wife as his possession. It was clear from the story she shared with me that Jack felt alienated and worried that he would not be able to survive in the UK. His behaviour was in part founded on his traditional beliefs that a man is superior to a woman and a wife should follow the instructions of her husband. But Mary and I think it was more than this: exerting control over Mary was a way of helping him feel better about his lack of success outside the home. The fact that he was not fulfilling his role as the provider, not able to find a job that matched his expectations, must have weighed heavily on him. The question asked by all those across cultures who research and write about domestic violence is why do men choose to take their frustrations out on women? The answer lies in how women's bodies are symbolically positioned in opposition to the male body and systematically devalued. The processes that operate to ensure women's inferiority to men, to maintain them as objects of control, are numerous and complex.

The stories told in this chapter challenge any assumptions that life in the UK is somehow miraculously better or easier that Zimbabwe. As Mary's story attests, if anything, women can feel more marginalised following migration. The traditional networks of church and female relatives which my mother accessed and which enabled her to leave a violent marriage were not available to Mary. Had she remained in Zimbabwe she would likely not have suffered in the same way and for so long. In the UK, unsurprisingly with a high concentration in London, there are many community-based organisations offering support services for asylum seekers and refugees. With regard to UK-based Zimbabwean organisations, their agenda tends to be largely political. The UK diaspora now exerts significant influence over changes that are occurring in Zimbabwe. The largest diaspora organisation, which includes in its remit a campaign against domestic violence, is the Zimbabwe Women's Network (http://www. zimwomenuk.org.uk/index.html). The Zimbabwe Women's Network was set up in 2003 to focus on the issues concerning the rights and welfare of Zimbabwean women refugees, asylum seekers, students and migrant workers and their families living in London, acknowledging the many challenges they face in the process of settlement and of integrating into the UK community. This organisation is transnational, with strong links to the network in Zimbabwe. In the process of writing this chapter I spent time researching what organisations exist in London specifically focusing on domestic violence among the Zimbabwe diaspora. I found none. Although some may exist – my research was not exhaustive – the issue of domestic violence does not seem to be a key priority. My concern is that my community does still not acknowledge the extent of the problem; domestic violence is still regarded as a private matter. The volumes reviewed at the start of this chapter also attest that whilst we know more now than ever about what the diaspora is doing and the experiences of different groups and individuals within it, domestic violence is not part of the discussion. Although Zimbabwean women in the UK can access services outside of the diaspora, many women, as Mary did, will find this hard and fear that secular, cross-cultural services will not understand them. Whilst this may in practice be a false assumption, secular services have to hear these fears and try to allay them. I hope this chapter serves to highlight the gaps in both research and practice, and that groups and networks within the diaspora can begin now to form to face this issue, moving it more squarely into the public arena where it can challenged.

5

Narratives of Divorce amongst Bangladeshi Women Living in England

Noorjahan Begum

This chapter documents the stories of three Bengali women who live in Tower Hamlets. The stories told here focus on their experiences of divorce but begin in each case with the deterioration of their marriages into violence. These stories are not meant to evoke feelings of sadness towards these women but bring out their courage and determination to navigate their way through their violent marriages and into a stronger and more positive existence. The stories highlight the centrality of marriage as the foundations of a Muslim way of life and emphasise the extent to which women are held responsible for maintaining it at all costs. The violent behaviour of each husband is attributed, by members of the Bengali community in Tower Hamlets and the religious leadership, to them 'losing their way', and not in the first instance considered a serious enough reason for the wife to leave. Furthermore, this explanation removes the husband in each case from direct responsibility for his failings which are linked to the temptations of the wider secular society which has enticed them into bad habits. Whilst the behaviour of violent husbands is attributed to inner weaknesses, some of the responses the women received from those whose advice they sought revealed an underlying belief that the use of violence towards wives was normal and even permissible if the woman had failed to fulfil her role adequately. This view is not universally voiced by the Bengali community – thankfully, many voices contest it – but it certainly comes through in some of the responses the storytellers in this chapter received.

This chapter will begin with an overview of Bengali marriage and divorce practices and review research examining how these practices are observed by the diaspora communities in the UK. The second section will present the life stories of the three women interviewed, focusing specifically on their lives from the point of marriage through to their divorces. In the third and last section, critical reflections will be given on the difficulties and reason for them that Bengali women face in the UK.

Bengali marriage in the Islamic context

Bengali marriage consists of a whole series of customs developed to reflect and endorse Islamic beliefs and practice. Bengali marriage begins with the practice of *stle* during which contact is initiated between the potential bride and groom and their families. During this ceremony gifts are given and food eaten. The function of the *stle* is for an official date to be set for both families to meet; this negotiation is done through a mutual contact, someone who acts as mediator. The first meeting of both families is known as a *cinepan* and it is the groom's family that visits the bride in her home with her family. During the *cinepan* both families discuss their expectations of each other and of married life; they will share something of their perspective on life and the values and principles that are important to them. This sharing of information acts as a further way of confirming the suitability of the match. Also during the *cinepan* both parties will work out what *mahr* should be paid. *Mahr* is a material gift given by the groom to the bride at the point of marriage. *Mahr* could be money or land either at home or abroad, gold jewellery or other consumer goods. *Mahr* should not be confused with dowry, a south Asian marriage practice sometimes also observed by Muslim familes. Dowry in the context of Hindu diaspora families is discussed in Chapter 6 of this volume. Dowry operates in reverse to *mahr* in that money and/or material goods flows from the bride's family to the groom's at the point of marriage and has been harshly criticised for reducing women to an economic commodity (see Bradley and Tomalin, 2009). *Mahr* is viewed by some commentators as a more positive practice for women as it recognises women's right to financial independence and operates as an assurance: should the marriage fail the bride can use her *mahr* to set up a new life for herself. *Mahr* therefore offers women a degree of financial independence. However, as with any religious and cultural practice, it still operates within an overarching patriarchal structure which leaves it open to abuse. In the final story told in this chapter, *mahr* was of positive benefit, allowing the storyteller to escape a violent marriage; it helped to secure her exit.

During the *cinepan* the costs of the wedding are allocated to each family and a date for the main ceremony finally set. The most important part of the wedding ceremony is the *nikkah* which is conducted by a religious leader from the community, usually from the local mosque. The *nikkah* is regarded as a solemn and a sacred contract, entered by both the bride and groom, whereby both parties have the freedom to define the terms and conditions of their marriage. The giving of *mahr* is a prerequisite of the marriage contract being formalised through the *nikkah*; it is considered essential for the groom to provide his bride with this gift, as it says in the Quran, 'And give the women [on marriage] their mahr as a nikkah [free gift]' (Quran, 4:4). *Mahr* is highlighted as a central part of Bengali marriage and must be settled before the other parts of the marriage contract can be agreed. Bengali Muslims in the UK strictly observe *mahr*, which also carries symbolic meaning representing the commitment and responsibility of the husband in relation to his wife. The level of *mahr* is not specified, but must be in moderation according to the groom's income. The *mahr* may be paid to the bride at the time of marriage or deferred to a later date, or a combination of both, all of which must be agreed prior to the finalisation of the *nikkah*.

The *nikkah* is concluded with the utterance of *ijab*, which is the consent given by the families for the bride and groom to enter into marriage, which is then followed by the expression of *qubul* or acceptance by the bride and groom of the responsibility that comes with marriage. The contract is finalised and written and then signed by the bride and the groom in front of two witnesses. The completion of the process is then announced publicly to the combined wedding parties in attendance at the *nikkah*. Following the *nikkah* is the reception at which many more guests will come and eat and celebrate the marriage. As described, *nikkah* is a marriage contract, one that is carefully pieced together and the implications and responsibilities explained to both the bride and groom. The wife is honoured through the gifting of *mahr* which also acts as her security should things go wrong. Despite the process through which *nikkah* takes place, in which the rights of the bride are equally respected, the stories below reveal three accounts in which husbands failed to conform to the contract they signed.

Patriarchal values still underpin the *nikkah* because bound up in the roles and responsibilities men and women are expected to assume in marriage are gendered ideals that render a women inferior in her domestic role to that of her husband who must provide. The *mahr* could be seen as a symbol of this role: the groom gives provides his wife with *mahr* as he then must provide for her through life. Patriarchy still shapes the contract endorsing male dominance in marriage which then in some instances legitimises a husband's violent and/or abusive behaviour. There is nothing unique about this pattern: religious practices are underpinned by patriarchal values that in turn shape gendered expectations in marriage, which prescribes an inferior role to women, leaving them more vulnerable to abuse and marginalisation. As already reviewed in the Introduction, all traditions similarly endorse a chain of events which ends with women struggling to navigate their marginal positions. Patriarchy is not just promoted through religion – secular society also finds ways to embed clear messages about gender that have similar effects. What these stories highlight is that in these cases including religion as part of the analysis does help to understand them. It also reveals how the *nikkah* can still, despite its foundations, be used by women to highlight their abuse and to bring justice to bear on husbands who fail to respect them after marriage. Community leaders and religious figures are called upon to uphold the principles of *nikkah* and although reluctance to support a woman leaving marriage is often expressed, her safety and right to respect and dignity is conveyed. This reaction and the principles of the marriage contract do also present possible solutions that the secular state could support in efforts to confront the abuse of women in the Bengal community.

In sharing stories from women in my community I hope to present an optimistic picture of how abuse and injustice is and can be challenged. The situation for many Bengali women may at least in part be shaped by their religious and cultural environment, but their wider marginalisation also reflects the failings of a the secular state to understand and work through appropriate responses. However, the solutions can also be found within our everyday lives.

The life stories of three Bengali women

Parveen's story

My first respondent is a forty-eight-year-old Bangladeshi housewife. She is currently surviving on state benefits and lives in a council house with her five children. She has been married for twenty-nine years but separated for eleven of those years. She was only recently served a petition for divorce as her estranged husband is looking to get married to his long-term girlfriend of thirteen years with whom he has been cohabiting for much for this time. He is also of Bangladeshi origin, aged fifty-five. He used to be a popular *bhola* singer, but his current occupation is unknown. Parveen, described to me how she was married in Bangladesh, after her husband went to visit her relatives and formally agreed to the marriage. She came from a prestigious family who owned vast amounts of land. They had been introduced through one of her relatives. After five years of marriage Parveen was finally able to join her husband in the UK. Prior to this point her husband had been reluctant to process the legal paperwork but he was placed under pressure by his family. They went on to have five children, ranging from twenty-nine to nineteen years old, three boys and two girls.

It was not long after arriving in the UK that Parveen's husband began to regularly abuse her, often violently. He frequently drank alcohol and became aggressive and would beat Parveen in front of their children. Parveen recalls how her husband 'came in and out of our lives. Sometimes a few years went by without a word, till one day, he'd turn up and demand to see the children.' He would force the youngest child to open the door while Parveen was out. He would intimidate the children until they let him into the residence and then wait for

Parveen to return. Her husband would then threaten and abuse her until she gave in to his pleas. Even while separated from her husband Parveen became pregnant several times, the last time being ten years ago when she had a stillbirth. Throughout this traumatic time Parveen did not seek a divorce, thinking, hoping that her husband would change his ways and return to her. Throughout her married life in the UK Parveen knew her husband was having a string of affairs and one relationship with a woman whom he regarded as his girlfriend. His relationship with this other woman was well known and Parveen's uncle found the spouse in bed with other women.

Eventually, Parveen consulted elders from her family, such as her father, uncle and brothers, who advised against seeking divorce. She described the reasons she was given by the elders: that she had five children and had to set an example; that society was very cruel to single mothers – gossip and malicious rumours would start and in turn it would be impossible for her to secure good marriages for her daughters, placing their futures in danger. Divorce, she was told, places women in a negative light, where they are stigmatised and children labelled negatively as damaged because they are seen as being from a broken home. Parveen felt it was better to live with the occasional visits from her husband and try to hide her status as a separated woman rather than live with the label 'divorced woman'. Eventually the community found out that Parveen was separated, and she was subjected to stigma and rumour; her behaviour came under scrutiny and suggestions were made that she was somehow to blame for chasing her husband away. However, despite the harassment she suffered she was still told by community elders that separation was better than divorce.

Parveen sought the advice of religious leaders but she found them unhelpful. They advised that she should 'give her husband time to see the error of his ways'. Throughout the years her husband disappeared, Parveen lived with her uncle and his family. Later the same uncle assisted her in squatting in a council flat; afterwards the council gave them full tenancy. Her uncle was supportive, took her to hospital, arranged school and helped her navigate the benefit systems. When Parveen first came to the UK she spoke no English; throughout the years she has attended ESOL classes and become more independent.

She has also moved into other council accommodation – a four-bedroomed house. Eventually, she found part-time work as a machinist.

Her eldest son at twenty-one divorced after marrying a 'white girl and getting her pregnant'; he now lives back at home. Her second eldest daughter got pregnant and has a daughter aged seven, remaining unmarried. Parveen agreed to adopt her granddaughter after her daughter put her child up for adoption. Another of her sons qualified and now works as a teacher. Another of her daughters is married with three children; she is a housewife with a 'supportive husband'. Her youngest and fifth child passed his A-levels with good grades, which Parveen is very proud of.

At the beginning of 2010 Parveen finally received a petition for divorce, instigated by the estranged husband. She was initially shocked: she had barely seen her husband in ten years and had given up on the idea that he would divorce her. She sought the advice of family members and was counselled by her uncles and other prominent community leaders that she agree to it; after all, they had been separated a long time and the children were now grown up.

Parveen expressed anger when talking about her divorce; she said she felt cheated. Those to whom she had turned for support when she had endured violence, abuse and abandonment at the hands of her husband for many years advised her to stay with him despite his behaviour and lack of financial support. Yet, as soon as her husband pushed for a divorce they advised her to take it. She feels she wasted much of her life on a man who abused her. Parveen feels like she lived for her children and now that she is older, she may never settle, may never find happiness for herself. She talks of her sadness and of feeling emotionally withdrawn from society. She claims she will always feel out of place in the UK and is mostly isolated. Although she does have a few friends who visit her, they are all so busy with their families they have very little time.

Parveen, after consulting with religious leaders, plans to keep her *mahram*. They have suggested she keep it since none of what has happened in the breakdown of the marriage is her fault. Her husband is the one who is seeking divorce so she is therefore entitled to the wealth accumulated through what marriage they had. This *mahram* will provide her with at least some security and peace of mind that what she has is hers. Parveen ponders why those she had consulted had shifted their views and perceptions compared to when she first sought counsel from them. She states that the 'religious leaders have now been replaced with those that have studied the *Shariah* more extensively. Therefore, they provide better advice in compliance with the *Shariah*. Family and the community have changed their perception through undergoing similar experiences, either by themselves or by someone close to them.' This more educated and considered approach is one of the most significant shifts she has witnessed since she migrated to the UK. She believes that this is a positive step for Bengali women, offering them hope that a way out of abusive marriages is now possible.

Amina's story

The second story documented in this chapter is that of a younger forty-year-old woman who works in commissioning. She divorced her first husband after twelve years of marriage and remarried after seven years to a man of Pakistani origin; they have now been together for two years. The couple met during a university open day and after dating for a year they decided to get married. After consulting with their respective families they were married. Amina finished her university studies and her husband worked for the Bank of England. Later her husband left this job and started working for the public sector. After six years of marriage Amina had a daughter. Following the birth of her child Amina also got a public sector job in the same building as her husband. While working she was liaising with different departments within the borough, and during this time she worked closely with a male colleague which her husband became uncomfortable about. Her husband did not like this colleague and did not get on with him; he was unhappy that his wife worked so closely with him. Amina's husband told her to leave her job because he did not want her spending so much time with this male colleague. Amina refused to leave and this marked the turning point in their marriage which then became tense.

As she continued working at the same job, she started hearing of her husband's afternoon lunches with various females from the department. This unsettled her and she started thinking that the main reason he did not want her to work in the same office was in fact his fear that he would be uncovered rather than genuine concerns about her fidelity working with a male colleague. As time progressed, her husband started getting aggressive in his pleas for her to stop working and on occasion mentioned that she was changing and becoming more independent, which he did not appreciate. Eventually he became very paranoid and started accusing her of having an affair with the colleague he considered as his rival. He started sending malicious emails around the department about this male colleague. After much slandering the male colleague felt pressured into leaving the department, taking employment elsewhere. This did not, however, end the pressures Amina experienced. Her husband still argued that she should leave her job in order to be a full-time housewife. Amina had, during this period of tension over her male colleague, been promoted and now held a management position she was reluctant to leave. She now earned more than her husband and wielded greater authority than he in the workplace.

As time progressed, Amina's husband continued to try to undermine her and control the family's finances. He tried to seize assets which Amina held prior to her marriage to him, including properties and a share in a restaurant business. He placed immense pressure on her to pay more of the household bills. He even had her sign legal documents, the significance of which Amina was not aware. She later found out they related to the handover of the properties to him. Now realising what he had done, she confronted him. Her husband's response was that this was necessary procedure and it was therefore for her own good. She also discovered that her husband secretly visited the restaurant which she had a share in and took a cut of the income which he never shared with her.

Throughout the four years he accused her of having affairs and being neglectful of their child and the home. Amina felt that she maintained well her role as mother, wife and homemaker, juggling home responsibilities with her career. She would also put herself out hosting her husband's family and mother. She recounted all the activities she took her daughter to as evidence of her good mothering, obviously feeling she needed to prove it because it was often doubted. She recounted how while she attended her daughter's performances and assemblies and organised birthday parties, her husband took a back seat. She felt that despite working she had built up a close relationship with her daughter and took the decision to work part-time so she could spend more time with her.

Her husband's slandering and jealousy grew in intensity. He started calling her family, telling them she was having an affair with her colleague. He became very paranoid and aggressive and on occasions became violent. When she told her family she had left her husband, her family initially thought it would all go back to normal, but after a few months had passed and she still lived apart from him they encouraged her to go back to him, as he was very persistent and was still pursuing her. Yet he was slandering Amina to her family members and friends and even relatives whom he barely spoke to. Amina found the scrutiny under which she was having to live because of the rumours he spread unbearable at times. She became very fragile and attempted suicide but was unsuccessful. Despite her psychological fragility her family still maintained that he was her husband and she should go back to him – not to do so would bring shame on her family and especially her daughter. Her daughter would find it difficult to find a good marriage match as she would be labelled in the same way as her mother, as flawed and dishonourable. It was also suggested that Amina's failure to return to her husband would affect her sisters' chances of finding good husbands; they too would be thought of as problems with flawed characters.

Eventually Amina went to seek legal advice, even after her father and brothers told her not to. This caused friction between Amina and her family, as they refused to come to terms with the fact that her marriage had failed; they maintained that she should go back to her husband. Her ex-husband persistently rang her and visited her, trying to get her to change her mind, but Amina refused to. He also continued to use violence to try to force her into coming back. In one instance he visited her flat and became very aggressive and violent, pinning her up against the wall with such aggression that he left finger marks on her throat. She filed a police report, and was put in touch with a domestic violence liaison officer, who assisted her throughout the case proceedings. However, this charge was later dropped due to lack of evidence. Amina believes that her ex-husband then vandalised her car and broke into her house on numerous occasions, expressing his continued grievances with her which seemed only to have been heightened by the court proceedings. Amina has had to attend custody hearings as her husband contested her right to look after their daughter. Amina spent four years going back and forth to court, until it was decided by the court that her daughter spend every other weekend and half of all holidays with the father.

Amina attributes the nervous break-down which she subsequently suffered and the emotional and psychological difficulties she has endured to the stress of all these experiences and to being away from her daughter for periods of time.

Finally, after a year of pushing, she was granted her English divorce, and at a later stage her Islamic divorce came through. However, the *Shariah* would only grant the divorce once the law of the land had dissolved the marriage. Amina felt that the Shariah Council still took a long time granting the divorce and she had to pay considerable money in order to complete the divorce process. The Council concluded, due to the grounds for their divorce, that it was reasonable for the respondent to keep her *mahr* money and gold, as her ex-husband had acted unreasonably during their marriage.

With time, and with help from family members and professionals, Amina has managed to overcome her psychological problems and is now working in a high management position in the public sector. She is also happily remarried.

Nadia's story

Nadia met her ex-partner at college, at the age of sixteen; he was seventeen. They dated each other for six years before getting married. He was the eldest child in a family of six; she was the seventh child out of a family of eight. Immediately after their marriage they lived with his family for six months until they received an offer for a one-bedroom flat which they then moved into.

Within a short time of moving to the flat Nadia's husband started coming home late, often not turning up for days; this created conflict between them. When confronted by Nadia about his whereabouts, he would get defensive, aggressive and occasionally became physically violent. In fits of rage he would throw things at her. Nadia recalls one instance when he threw a vase, other occasions when he beat her, giving her a bloody nose. Once, he beat her so strongly that he broke his own finger. When Nadia did tackle her husband over his violence he just responded by saying that she had no choice but to endure it as she had chosen to marry him so it was her own fault. He often blamed her for his behaviour, claiming that is was the result of her 'nagging'. For a year, Nadia kept his violence a secret from her friends and family.

A year into the violence Nadia's husband lost his job due to his lack of attendance and punctuality; however, he kept this from Nadia for three months. She started to become suspicious when unpaid bills mounted up and a final notice came on their rent account. She then confronted him which led to one of the most violent outbursts she endured. After receiving a sustained beating her husband instructed her to go and ask her father for money, as he considered him wealthy and well positioned to help. Nadia did not go to her father as she did not want to disclose to to him her marital problems. She continued to live with violence as part of her everyday life, either actual or the fear of it. She felt unable to seek help because the marriage was not arranged but her choice, the culmination of a long-term relationship with someone she thought she knew and loved. She felt ashamed that she had misjudged him and had not been able to see that he was abusive. She worried that blame would be placed on her for going her own way and not seeking the advice and guidance of her parents through an arranged union.

The tipping point for Nadia was her pregnancy, throughout which the violence continued. Her husband still beat her, on one occasion so severely that an ambulance was called and she required hospitalisation. Nadia recalls the terror of being examined in hospital and the moment when the doctors could not find her baby's heartbeat during the ultra sound. She remained in hospital for eight hours and was given further tests. Eventually the medical professionals were happy the baby was still alive. Reflecting on how close she came to losing her baby served as a crude and brutal wake-up call for Nadia. She now had to face the severity of the violence her husband served to her. She took the important step of contacting her husband's family, specifically his uncle from whom she had received support through the years of her marriage. The uncle advised Nadia to leave her husband, implying that he was a drug addict, therefore, not in the correct state of mind and not safe to be around. Despite receiving this advice Nadia did not leave at this point but remained, believing that she could change her husband and help him through his addiction. She felt it was her duty to do this as his wife and soon-to-be mother of his child.

Surprisingly, for a brief period her husband was supportive and attentive, especially during the labour and birth of her son in hospital. Her husband carefully oversaw the observance of Islamic customs following the birth, including the shaving of the baby's head by the grandparents on the father's side; it was they who also named the child. Once this ritual was completed and the baby officially named, Nadia returned home – and almost immediately her husband became violent again. On the second night at home after giving birth, Nadia felt weak, experiencing post-labour pains which rendered her unable to stand, let alone care for her baby. Knowing that her son needed a nappy change and unable to do it herself she woke her husband, asking him to do it. Her husband immediately reacted violently and kicked her in the stomach and crotch, subjecting Nadia to agonising pain which went on for days and meant she could barely move. The next day, her husband showed remorse, apologised and promised to behave – but on the condition that she did not 'nag' him, which he still blamed for his violent outbursts. Reflecting on her experience, Nadia realises that she had internalised this blame and did feel in some way responsible for causing him to be violent; this more than any other factor explained why she did not leave him sooner. Without anyone close to her with whom she could talk about what was happening, she listened only to what her husband told her, believing it to be true.

Six weeks following the birth of her son, her husband threw a shoe at her which missed but landed on her baby. This was the final act.

Nadia asked her husband to leave, threatening to call the police if he did not. Her husband became agitated and violent, and Nadia was scared for her child and what might happen if she did not get him to leave. She then took the step to call the police who upon arrival promptly arrested her husband. He then spent a night in a cell before he was released.

The next day, Nadia received a call from the social services, who notified her that because her son was in the home during this violent outburst he would be placed on the child safety register and the home situation monitored. If there were any further reports of violence in the home, regardless of whether or not the child was hurt, it may be necessary to remove him for his safety.

This scared Nadia and she did not report any further incidents that occurred. This meant that she had to suffer in silence, as her child might be taken away or placed on the child safety register, then every time she took him to hospital for genuine reasons she might be reprimanded or suspicion would be raised.

Nadia feels that while her husband was away from her, it gave her time and strength to consider her future and her marriage. As her husband had no access, he was unable to sway her.

However, after three weeks, her husband returned home, apologised and promised not to behave in such a violent manner again. Nadia forgave him and even felt guilty that he had spent the night in a cell because she called the police. As had happened previously, neighbours would call the police when there was a disturbance, but now Nadia would deny that she was being abused. Therefore, her husband carried on without fear of repercussions.

However, after six months, Nadia's child, who at the time was crawling, came across a bag of weed. Nadia now realised that her husband had been under the influence of drugs all along and that his violent outbursts may have been due to long-term drug abuse. She finally realised that she had been living in a state of denial, believing each time that her husband would change. As she stared at the drugs she knew it was unlikely he would ever overcome his violence. Nadia at this moment made the decision to leave her marriage for the sake of her child and his future. Family members supported her decision to leave but urged her to think of it only as a temporary measure, giving her husband the space to get himself clean and free from a drug dependency. Nadia, however, could not look back and wanted to move beyond this part of her life and into a new path that she had control of and which was clear of any fear or guilt. She knew as soon as she left that she wanted a divorce.

After a little time she spoke with her immediate family – her father and mother and siblings – and told them how she felt. She received their support which then gave her the strength to file for a divorce. Other members of her family and the wider community held on for longer to the view that she should be open to the possibility of returning to her husband. These lingering views of a few, advising her to return, did not weigh that heavily on Nadia: once she had left she felt sure it was the right thing to do. However, the views expressed did evoke anger and a realisation that some of the beliefs of her culture did not protect women but clearly operated to preserve the superiority of men. For example, members of the community who sought to advise her during her separation, prior to her divorce, stated that it was not uncommon for husbands to be violent and that often wives deserved this. In numerous conversations Nadia was told that women sometimes 'need to be taught a lesson', and that 'women should endure what fate holds for them'. Additionally, she was advised that she may find it difficult to ever remarry, and could therefore be facing the rest of life alone, the implication being that marriage at any cost is better than living the life of a single woman.

Nadia was not able to easily leave her married life and its traumas behind; throughout the divorce proceedings her husband harassed her and often became aggressive and threatening in an attempt to get her to change her mind and return to him. He refused to cooperate so the divorce proceedings dragged out, making it difficult for Nadia to move on with her life. Finally, a year later, the decree absolute was granted. However, Nadia's husband refused to accept the secular divorce and continued to refer to her as his wife. He insisted that the divorce be carried out according to the *Shariah*, which meant that advice had to be sought from the Shariah Council at the Mosque. This process of consultation with male clerics was stressful; it again became clear that the system was stacked against women. The Council members pushed her to rethink her actions, suggesting that she had not done enough to save her marriage and that this was her ultimate duty. However, Nadia feels that it is not the *Shariah* Law that imposes on women, but the men who implement the *Shariah*, as she feels it is in their best interest to side with the men, as this will maintain women's social role and discourage them from leaving their husbands.

Islamic divorce proceedings

In the UK, Islamic divorces are carried out through the Shariah Council, whereby all proceedings are required to be in accordance with the Quran and the 'Sunnah' of the prophet Mohammed. The Shariah Council can only grant a divorce if a civil divorce has been granted through the British legal system. However, if no civil marriage was carried out, then the Shariah Council may grant a divorce. There are two types of divorce. One is instigated by a husband though a process called *talaq*, whereby the husband utters the divorce verbally, in front of witnesses, in a calm state. The *mahr* may then be kept by the wife as an act of kindness and as a payment. This is then processed by the Shariah Council, based on the individual's circumstances. The second type of divorce, known as *khula*, occurs when a woman petitions for it. The general consensus is that a woman who seeks divorce should return her *mahr* to her husband in exchange for his agreement to the divorce. If a husband refuses his wife's divorce, the wife is able to apply for a *khula*, providing there are reasonable grounds for divorce. If the *khula* is granted, the newly divorced woman must agree to *iddat*, which is a waiting period before she embarks upon another marriage.

What do these stories reveal?

Nadia was able to begin her life again in part because her immediate natal family supported her decision to leave; she was also helped by the provision of *mahr*, awarded at the point of marriage to a woman as an insurance in case she finds herself alone. Despite knowing that leaving was possible, in that she had sufficient funds to start again, Nadia did not leave until a final tipping point. In each case the woman sought support and advice from within her immediate family, including that of her husband, and also from members of the wider Bengali community. This advice – despite outrage at the behaviour of the husband – was against the wife leaving the marriage. The preservation of the marriage was placed above the personal safety of each woman, and in each case later also of their children. Interventions from those whose counsel was sought was limited and non-radical, leaving each woman to continue to endure her violent marriage until they each faced the reality that nothing would change whilst they remained in them. The individuals whose intervention and support was given were predominantly men. It is perhaps unsurprising that they had a vested interest in maintaining the patriarchal foundations of marriage which focus primarily on the wife's responsibilities towards her family, caring for them and managing the domestic sphere of life. In the last case, the *Shariah* clerics expressed reluctance in granting Nadia her divorce, insistent that she continue to try to make the marriage work. Nadia and Amina feel the truth of their religion has been distorted by male application of teachings surrounding marriage and divorce. For each woman, her religious identity is of primary importance and in no way do they find the teachings of Islam to blame for their experiences of violent marriages. The problem rests with the male domination of the process of practically translating teachings into everyday life.

Although there are, so each woman claims, female leaders at a local level, women who have acquired respect from within the community and whose advice is valued and sought, there are far more men who assume this position. When problems first materialise it is to these community figures that women and their families turn. In each story religious leaders came into the picture at a much later stage, once the divorce had been asked for, and their involvement often slowed the process down. None of the woman whose stories are told here accessed the advice and support from specialist services aimed at responding to the specific needs of Bengali women. When asked why they did not seek such support, each woman replied simply that they did not know of any such agencies. But it was also the case that the traditional way of responding to a marriage situation was to turn first to your family and then other members of the community. This tendency to turn inwards to navigate problems is perhaps intensified by the disporic experience of being marginal to the secular masses. It may also be due to a belief that marriage is such a central part of what it is to be Bengali Muslim that no one outside of this culture could appreciate the significant impact of divorce. However, these explanations do not account for the lack of community-level networks through which women can access support from others whose experiences are similar. The secular state has clearly failed to nurture and support the growth of these more indigenously rooted and culturally responsive services, which in turn contributes to the continued marginalisation of women and means that many remain in violent situations much longer than they wish, unable to draw on the validating support needed to make the move towards divorce.

These stories, once again, as with the chapters preceding, reveal the underlying legitimisation of violence against women utilised as a mechanism to limit the mobility of women. The use of violence in this way is indiscriminative in that women across class and wealth groups are equally affected and equally find it difficult to leave. Education and financial security are not enough to give a woman the confidence and determination to leave. Above all else, support is the key factor: support from those who understand what the woman has suffered and can offer assurances that divorce and a new life is worth achieving.

6

Transnational Accounts of Dowry and Caste: Hindu Women Tell Their Stories

Charlenie Naik

Many people will have heard stories about oppressed, downtrodden Hindu wives. The images these stories invoke have helped to form stereotypical preconceptions of Indian women as victims of their culture, silenced, unable to challenge the restrictions placed upon them. I, from a young age growing up in a *Brahmin* family in Manchester, have been concerned and frustrated by the conventions of my religion and culture, reinforced by the restrictions of the caste system. Raised in a Hindu household, I have often found myself fighting against the gender role and the expectations of my culture. I have been brought up to prepare myself for marriage; as a *Brahmin* woman I am expected to get a good education including a degree as this will make me attractive to prospective husbands. Once married I am expected to observe the duties of a wife and then in time a mother. Despite the success of my *Brahmin* community – the business prosperity and academic achievements – the social expectations seem to have been sustained through generations and across continents almost intact.

This chapter is a compilation of the oral narratives of a group of four *Brahmin* women, first- and second-generation migrants here in the UK. I have asked my storytellers to focus on caste, marriage and the practice of dowry, which occurs prior to marriage. Very little is known about how dowry is practised in the UK and, as stated in the Introduction to this volume, it has to a large extent managed to go on under the radar of government. Yet in India, feminists hold it responsible for a host of atrocities against women. Southall Black Sisters have stated that dowry is part of numerous cases they encounter in the UK, and Hannana Siddiqui intertwines this into the stories she analyses in her chapter. The lack of information regarding the impact of dowry on women's lives in the UK needs urgently to be addressed – as my conversations documented in this chapter attest, women believe it helps to support notions of female inferiority. This chapter will serve two objectives. Firstly, I will explore my own internal conflicts with the patriarchal Hindu system, which I know to be shared by many Hindu women my age, and compare these experiences with those of the older generation. I will ask: has anything changed for *Brahmin* women? Has migration to the UK made any difference to the choices we have? The second objective is to analyse the role which dowry and caste play in transmitting patriarchal expectations, ensuring women's compliance to marriage and domesticity.

All the women whose stories are recorded in this chapter were chosen to participate because they hold family relations, and all were happy for me to record their conversations with each other about dowry and the changing contexts of their lives. All the women were born into the same high caste. Their stories weave together as the conversations they share with me and one another develop into an analysis of the role and status of *Brahmin* women in the UK. The Hindu caste system is equivalent to class structures in other countries, except that this Indian system has been rigidly enforced and has persisted for thousands of years. The caste system was enforced as law throughout the subcontinent until the adoption of the Indian constitution in 1949, which outlawed it. Nevertheless, the caste system remains a deeply ingrained social structure, particularly in rural India and among the Hindu diaspora in Britain today.

As I have already stated, I asked the women to focus in their conversations on dowry and its implications for their lives. Before I go any further I need to unpack what dowry is and what it means in the context of south Asian Hindu culture. Tomalin (2009) states: 'It is difficult to provide a precise definition of dowry since it has undergone distinct transformations over time, and it can encapsulate a range of different practices of marital gift-giving.' Tomalim cites the work of

Srinivasan and Lee (2004: 1108) who suggest that dowry in India grew from a number of different ritual exchanges:

> The dowry system – payments from the bride's family to the groom or groom's family at the time of marriage – has a long history in India and other Asian societies ... The modern Indian dowry system has its roots in the traditional upper-caste practices of *kanyadhan* (literal meaning: gift of the virgin bride), *varadakshina* (voluntary gifts given by the bride's father to the groom), and *stridhan* (voluntary gifts given by relatives and friends to the bride) ... Traditionally, although these gifts could be significant, they were often small tokens of good wishes. More recently, however, the dowry has come to involve a substantial transfer of wealth from the bride's family to the groom's, and has become a major factor in marriage negotiations. (Quoted by Tomalin, 2009: 1.)

In this chapter I capture how the women I spent time with understand the impact that both their caste identity and dowry has had on their lives. Their stories confirm that dowry is prevalent in the UK where, unlike India, there is no legislation protecting women from the repercussions, post-marriage, that this practice is known to cause. The chapter is divided into two parts: firstly I review the link between caste, gender and dowry; summarising key research but also offering my own reflections on how I feel patriarchal gender ideology has affected me; secondly I look at the life stories and conversations I had with four *Brahmin* women. I conclude by summarising the most important factors I feel my research has highlighted.

Caste, gender and dowry

Caste

There are four main castes or *varnas* into which everyone is categorised. At the very top are the *Brahmins* – the priests, scholars and philosophers. The second highest caste is the *Kshatriyas* – these are the warriors, rulers, and those concerned with the defence and administration of the village or state. Third comes the *Vaishyas*, who are traders, merchants and people involved in agricultural production. The lowest caste is the *Shudras* – the labourers and servants for the other castes. Each caste includes many hierarchical sub-castes divided by occupation known as *jati*. The *varna* and *jati* systems operate in parallel. The *varna* (class) system is thought to have emerged out of the *Rig Veda* (ancient rituals) and specifically from the sacrificing of a man known as Purusha:

> When they divided the Man, into how many parts did they apportion him?
>
> What do they call his mouth, his two arms and thighs and feet?
>
> His mouth became the Brahmin, his arms were made into the Warrior, his thighs the People, and from his feet the Servants were born. (*Rig Veda*)

These two verses come from a famous hymn describing Purusha's sacrifice, the *Purusha Sukta,* which is found in the *Rig Veda.* The *Purusha Sukta* contains the first mention of the four *varnas* of Hindu society. The association between the four *varnas* and parts of Purusha's body establishes a hierarchy that attributes greater prestige to the *Brahmins* coming from his mouth and the lowest to the *Shudras* associated with Purusha's feet. Those who find themselves lying outside the caste system have throughout Indian history been subjected to extreme discrimination and labelled 'untouchables'. Under the leadership of Dr Ambedkar, himself born into an untouchable family, a movement opposed to caste emerged, Ambedkar fought for the term *dalit* (outcaste) to replace untouchable. In 1950 Ambedkar succeeded in getting legislation through the Indian parliament to protect the human rights of all *dalits*.[1]

Despite the current provision in the Indian constitution designed to protect the rights of *dalits* and the reservations allocated to ensure that those in this group have opportunities, the hierarchal divisions of Indian society are still apparent and have transplanted themselves to the UK. Male *Brahmins* emerged as scholars privileged with education that enabled them to read the epics and write others such as the *Dharmashastra*, outlining the duties and responsibilities of people according to their caste and also gender. The specific duties and responsibilities for women are detailed in the *Stridharma* and they clearly associate women with the domestic sphere. Teltumbde (2010) argues that the persistence of caste relates to the concern of the privileged elite to preserve their power. To be of a high caste brings not just prestige but opportunities. *Brahmins* are reluctant to relinquish the status and all it brings. The reluctance of *Brahmins* to relinquish this power is at the heart of the continued replication of this form of social organisation.

Gender and Hinduism

Despite being born into a *Brahmin* family I do not feel I have much power to carve out a drastically different life for myself other than that prescribed by my parents, which in turn has come from theirs. Ideas about how we should live our lives are inherently gendered, but where do these ideas come from? I have already traced the origins of the caste system to the *Rig Veda*; concepts of gender also emerge out of religious texts. One of the first scholars to argue that religious texts have an impact on social and cultural reality was Julia Leslie. A classical Indologist working with Sanskrit texts, one of Leslie's most cited works is *The Perfect Wife* (1989) in which she translates the *Stridharmapaddhati* of Tryambakayajvan, a text that outlines the role of 'orthodox' Hindu women. She argues that texts both impact on social life and voice a commentary on it, and further that within Hinduism, some texts offer guidance and knowledge, setting out how Hindus should approach their day-to-day lives. So how then do these texts help to shape and promote practices such as dowry, that in itself is not a religious practice? Scholars such as Leslie articulated the ways in which patriarchal religion establishes gender inequalities that can then allow dowry and dowry-related violence to flourish. An example of this patriarchal gender ideology can be seen in the differentiation between the purpose of women's and men's lives which strictly binds women's roles to the domestic sphere. Dowry can be understood as a mechanism that reflects as well as serves to further embed this ideology in the lives of women.

Texts such as the *Laws of Manu* (Doniger 1991) and the *Stridharmapaddhati* of Tryambakayajvan directly list the roles and responsibilities of women. In *The Perfect Wife* Leslie stresses the importance of linking texts to the social reality ubiquitous both at the time the texts were produced and today. In her last article before her untimely death in 2004, *Gender and Hinduism* (2005), Leslie affirms that religious texts hold significant influence in shaping cultural and social environments, and ancient Hindu texts clearly promote a gender ideology which is still in existence today. Although many texts may have diminished in prominence, they have left a lasting imprint on the social and cultural fabric of women's lives. Few people today read texts such as the *Stridharmapaddhati* of Tryambakayajvan, but they have contributed to the creation of an enduring social environment within which female oppression has become normalised. Bradley and Tomalin state:

> We are not arguing that 'dowry murder' or dowry as a cultural product are Hindu practices as such, but rather that there are features of Hinduism that sustain views about women that play a role in shaping social institutions that can serve to normalise discrimination as well as violence against women. There is no linear and straightforward relationship between religion and dowry and the problems associated with it, but there are links between religious values and institutions, and practices that discriminate against and marginalize women. (2009: 2)

Theologians argue that religion plays a part in both sustaining discriminatory heterosexual marriage practices and also the normalisation of violence against women (Bradley, 2010; Hawthorne, 2004; King and Beattie, 2004; Puttick, 1998; McIntosh, 2007). As stated in the Introduction to this volume, King argues that religion must, therefore, form part of the critical analysis of all forms of oppression against women, since religions are predominantly, if not exclusively, shaped by male perspectives and experiences (King, 2005: 3298).

The relationships between religious traditions and misogynistic ideals, which in turn sustain an often hostile environment for women, have been identified across all religious traditions (King, 1995; Young, 1995; Young, Sharma and Young, 1991; King and Beattie, 2004). In the case of Hinduism its patriarchal values have produced, for example, a preference for sons and male succession, which clearly privileges the male subject, whereas women have been designated the role of caring and serving. Dowry arguably 'feeds' from these 'traditions', which aim to ensure that male needs and desires define and dominate women's lives and roles (see also Knott, 1996). These particular dimensions, which are prominent in Hinduism, can be identified as having contributed towards the social conditions that have allowed modern dowry practices to flourish, where there is an elevation of male authority and superiority underpinned by wifely submission, compliance and duty (or *stridharma*).

A balance needs to be found that understands the ways in which religion and culture weave together to support a chain of patriarchy, yet which does not reduce gender discrimination and its manifestations, such as dowry practices, to religious or cultural causes. The chain begins in Hinduism with son preference, heterosexual marriage and wifely submission, upon which modern dowry practices feed in many parts of India, leaving women vulnerable to dowry-related violence and also other forms of violence. Religion plays a part in securing the first links of this chain – evident from textual analysis of Hindu epics, for instance, or through anthropological studies of the role of women in Hindu society.

Understanding this complex nexus out of which dowry has emerged and manifests has helped me to appreciate why I often experience pressure from my family to conform to a traditional female role. Patriarchal gendered values are embedded into the very foundations of how my family lives their lives. Challenging the negative impact the values have on my life is important to me, though at the same time I wish to celebrate the positive aspects of my culture. My family is close knit which gives me a sense of security; I am close to them and know they love me.

As my stories reveal, the women with whom I spent time are open with each other, willing to express their emotions, perceptions and critical reflections with me and with one another. This network of support across generations provides support and counselling in bad times and I value it highly.

Navigating a 'double life'

As stated at the opening of the chapter, I feel the need to challenge the stereotypical presumptions people outside of my culture have about what living as a Hindu woman is like, in particular the view that we are all oppressed and with little voice to form autonomous choices. Whilst I do feel constrained by aspects of my upbringing, I am able to contest my parents' decisions about my future. I was raised in an Indian Hindu household, with two parents and two brothers. I am the middle child and only daughter. During my upbringing I have often found myself fighting against the particular gender role my parents (more my dad) assumed I would conform to. Subsequently, I have been equally concerned and frustrated by the conventions of my society, which I believe are exaggerated by the restrictions of the caste system. As a high-caste woman my behaviour outside the home is strictly monitored; these expectations conflict with Western secular values that offer me greater freedoms to participate in public life. Throughout my teenage years I found it particularly difficult to carve out my own sense of personhood and identity. I felt that I fell somewhere between my strict *Brahmin* upbringing and the liberal secular state that is my homeland. I know my experiences are shared by many BME women, and I feel the specific tensions and difficulties caused by navigating conflicting constructions of my identity remain relatively unrecognised by those outside this group. The state, government officials and policy makers do not focus on our everyday emotional traumas but on the more extreme end of the spectrum, that is, honour crimes and other graphic forms of gender-based violence.

The majority of second and third generation British Indians experience a 'double life'. Often amongst friends and relations, I have discussed this concept of almost living two separate lives; with different personalities adopted as we step between the wider secular society and the cultural values of our homes. We have little choice but to try and skilfully balance our two cultures, but frequently find ourselves criticised by traditional parents for 'losing our roots' or becoming 'too Westernised'. This intense scrutiny of my generation by elders causes significant conflict within close-knit British Indian communities, resulting in a host of consequences, sometimes fatal. The stories told in this chapter, across generations, focus on this tension between tradition and secularism. They also reveal the ways in which Indian women of my generation are pushing for change. We do not want to lose our heritage but we resist the patriarchal assumptions that we will conform to a submissive, domestic model of womanhood.

Stories of marriage, caste and dowry

I interviewed four women from across generations, from two related families, all from the Gujarati *Anavil* (honorary) *Brahmin* caste. Two of my interviews were conducted in Gujarati, thus I required a translator to ensure I retold the stories correctly in English. However, some meaning may well have been lost through this process of translation, but I hope the essence is still accurate. Generally, conducting this research did not pose too many problems. I visited most of my storytellers in their homes where I hoped they would be at most comfort. Beforehand, I made efforts to spend time with each person alone in order to make them feel confident with me and relaxed enough to give honest recollections. One of the storytellers came to my home so that she could speak to me away from her husband; she wanted to be able to liberally express her views and emotions and felt this would not be possible in front of him. Living amongst my storytellers the whole of my life, within the same wider multicultural community, meant I could to some degree empathise with them, and I hope this also helped them feel at ease. I have endeavoured to delve into my work with great objectivity, but as with the authors of the other chapters, I have personal and political reasons for conducting this research. All of my storytellers are given fictional names, protecting their anonymity. The four glimpses given here reveal instances of cultural adaptation, experiences of isolation and violence, all sharing a common underlying restriction – that of patriarchy. I feel that through this research I have embarked upon an incredible journey during which I have learnt to appreciate the extent to which the lives of women in my community often weave together despite generational differences.

I start with the stories of two elderly Indian women who migrated to Britain during the late 1960s and early 1970s. Firstly, Shanti, an elderly woman born in the north-west region of Gujarat, was married during her early teenage years and later migrated to London during

1967 for a desired better way of life. Shanti later moved to Bolton with her family; years later eventually settling in Manchester, and now as a widow she lives in Leeds with her daughter-in-law and son. It is Hindu tradition that once a widow a woman goes to live with either her eldest or youngest son. Shanti is an extremely religious individual who performs *puja*[2] daily and had always throughout their upbringing tried to instil the importance of religious practice into her children. Her two daughters are highly successful professionals working in higher education as teachers in Manchester, and her son (with whom she now lives) is a medical doctor in Leeds. Shanti is very much autonomous in her attitude to life and forthright in her opinions. She regularly visits India, as for her it still remains her homeland despite the numerous years she has now been in the UK. These visits are important, she told me, as a way of affirming her cultural and religious identity.

The second lady, Bhakti, also now a widow, lives with her youngest son's family. Bhakti has close family ties with Shanti, both spending most of their lives living on the same street in Manchester. Bhakti and her husband migrated from India to Zambia to pursue a better quality of life as a result of increased opportunities in Africa. In Zambia they proudly raised four sons. Bhakti's late husband was a political activist, often protesting for the freedom of oppressed Indians in Zambia. Eventually Bhakti settled in Manchester with her children. Unlike Shanti, she does not feel the need to visit India and prefers her life in Britain, which she has grown to love. Bhakti finds her widow status liberating; she asserts herself as the matriarchal head of the household.

Bhakti and Shanti told me that they often compare notes on the patriarchal upbringing they had in Gujarat and feel that leaving India has enabled them to experience different values which have provided the chance for each of them to exert more control over day-to-day decision-making. However, such freedom was only really realised once they both became widows; until that point they both remained compelled to fulfil the expectations of a dutiful Hindu wife and mother. The status of widowhood in India is for many women oppressive (Knott, 1996), but for Shanti and Bhakti it has proved to open new doors. At the point of marriage for both women dowry was given, and although neither associated the practice with women's vulnerability they did talk about how they felt it carries certain assumptions about women's role and duties in marriage. Both women also agreed that they felt it was important for dowry to still be offered by a bride's family even in the UK; they saw it is a mark of respect between the two families. Shanti talked of giving dowry prior to her daughter's marriage as she wanted to make sure she knew she was loved. So the giving of money and goods for Shanti was a way of communicating to her daughter that she cared for and valued her.

The other stories are those of two Hindu women living in the north-west region of England. They are Krishna (second generation) and Parisa (first generation). Krishna is in her early thirties, born to traditional Hindu parents in Coventry, but now residing in Leeds. Krishna is fluent in spoken Gujarati and overtly displays her Indian cultural heritage by dressing in saris for formal occasions and participating in traditional Indian dance. She is also deeply proud of her Western upbringing, feeling it is important for her to pursue her career as an A-level teacher at a local college. She shared with me her frustrations at having to juggle the expectations she has for her life in terms of pursuing a career and at the same time feeling the pressure to conform to the dictates of being a dutiful Hindu wife. She talked of the obstacles she faced at the time of marriage which, as with the storytellers in Chapter 3, represent a real watershed in her life when the two cultures she had managed up to this point to keep apart, collided.

Parisa moved to Bolton at the age of eight and found herself in the role of mother to her younger brother and sister, after her mum became semi-disabled. Parisa took on the adult responsibility of cooking daily for her siblings and looking after their general well-being whilst juggling the demands of school life. She felt this experience forced her to mature mentally at a much faster rate; putting all her own needs secondary to those of her mother and siblings.

Although the caste system is not embedded into secular society in the UK, Parisa asserts how it has still impacted on her life. 'While the caste system is not a structural part of the societal framework here, it is still used as a reference for the women who were the first generation migrants such as myself. The caste system has had some impact on clearly demarcating people's roles specifically in relation to rituals and social etiquette which are different for each caste. As a result of migration, caste boundaries have to some extent become blurred; more marriages have taken place across castes groupings and this has resulted in less differentiation of rituals and social etiquette between groups. Inter-caste marriages are more popular, with the elders preferring marriages within the Indian community as opposed to other "extremes". Again, this last point is likely to impact much more on the females as they are still more strictly "policed" on such matters as going out, marriage, the way they have to behave in their marital home, although at the same time females today are given more freedom to move away to study, or live on their own. Women are able to work full time in most job areas they want without restriction and the younger generation in my opinion can now to some degree compete on an equal level to their white counterparts as well as the males in their society.'

Krishna explained the repercussion of the caste system in the UK: 'In some cases, those viewpoints are not left in the country when they leave; they [women born in India] then take them to wherever they go, and then because they talk about it, out of context probably, all Indians get a bad name.'

It was a view shared by Shanti and Bhakti – that women in their culture who married into a lower caste became immediately ostracised from the family. When caste mixing occurs, as Shanti remarks, 'females especially face trouble, people won't even allow their children to marry into their own caste. The children are only accepted into society because they have the mixed blood of the father.'

Although the caste system is eliminated in Britain, these etiquettes are still expected to be obeyed by the high castes, inferring that notions of the caste system remain prevalent in contemporary British Indian culture. Each caste upholds specific customs which need to be upheld in order to be accepted within their social circle. If a woman is to marry into a different caste, she won't have the required knowledge to participate in the rituals of that caste; her in-laws may even offer her the wrong advice. Problems can even arise in 'love marriages' of the same caste. During Bhakti's era there was an incident such as this, where the young girl's parents didn't approve of her marriage so they refused to even talk to their daughter. Later, when her dad passed away, her family even disallowed her to see him. Another story shared by Bhakti fell into the same context: 'I even know of a woman that married into the *Vaishya* caste and her parents moved away to another area; she and her new husband have moved all the way to Australia as the problem was never resolved.'

When women reach marital age it is expected that suitable partners will be found for them. Most often these matches represented 'marriages of convenience' for the family, ensuring family and caste ties remained strong. Prospective brides were left with very little if any say in who they might marry. In modern times this has changed, with people becoming more open minded and accepting. Matches now usually have to be agreed by both the potential bride and groom. However, patriarchal family arrangements still present many problems for Hindu women in the UK both before and after marriage. In some cases, and as Hannana in her chapter covers, women run away from marriages they feel will compromise their freedom, or in extreme cases, safety. Shanti reflected on the tensions arising through marriage: 'When two strong-minded people want to come to a decision, conflict will always occur.' She then recalled numerous stories from the1970s of struggles within families over the marriage of their children. A woman she knew ran away with her passport so she could marry a Pakistani boy. It was the norm for parents to keep their children's passports to prevent this from happening. Shanti shared another incident in which the marriage took place within the same caste, a Patel married a Mistry (caste can also be identified by surname), yet it still resulted in the daughter being disowned because they did not share the same sub-caste grouping. The daughter moved to Canada and only after her father died did her mother associate with her. Ironically, her only son married a white girl, and when this happened she had no option but to give in, as, Shanti recalls, 'she couldn't do anything about it'.

On some occasions, parents even feel the need to lie about their daughter's marriage. Shanti informed me of how an Indian girl wanted to marry an Iranian but her parents were devout Hindus. So they decided to tell everyone that he was Italian, since marrying a Muslim Iranian would bring humiliation and shame upon her family. Elaborating on the patriarchal structure of societal power, Shanti articulates what happened in the previous generation when all the family lived together in extended family stratification. 'When a women goes into the marital house she is expected to adapt to the family ... not only does the eldest brother have rule over the rest of the house and has to make the main decisions but he also keeps hold of all the money, rendering potential abuse of the income. This in turn causes problems with younger siblings and the rest of the extended family. This still happens today.'

Parisa reinforces Shanti's views: 'This definitely used to be the norm in India where the financial strength of the main patriarch held the family together and women were wholly dependent on the male for their economic and social well-being. When her husband died, a woman was left at the mercy of the other younger members of the family to look after her. Today, however, women in the upper class such as ours work full time in many cases and as such are economically independent and do not have to rely on the males in the family. As such they do not face the same constraints in this respect. However, the framework they have been brought up in (certainly the older generation) means they are held in constraint by the psychological frameworks that are imposed on them. Most highly educated and well brought up women still let their husbands take care of the financial aspects of their lives; their role is that of a homemaker, nurturing children and caring for the family throughout life. However, one point is certainly clear: that they are capable of coping financially alone, albeit difficult at first.'

Krishna shares a similar perspective to Parisa on patriarchal constraints: 'I think there is a lot of truth in that statement. However far up the female goes in the scheme of things there are still plenty of constraints on how well she can do. Women still have to be the carers in the family (for elderly people or children), and are still the major cleaners/cooks in the family. If a women earns more money than her husband it may hurt his sensibilities, so she must be sensitive to this. The latter is unfortunately true!'

When questioned about struggles around the patriarchal family arrangements, Parisa stated: 'Other than the financial demarcation of the roles between men and women, as long as these are adhered to then there are no major disputes. However, with the blurring of caste lines and women having opportunities to work in the UK, men, more than women, are finding it difficult to adjust to new social etiquette and values and often try to resist this change. Women may try to influence men and encourage them to change and become more liberal, but issues such as girls and relationships with boys are still very stilted; even with contraceptives the fear remains that girls will become pregnant outside marriage and the family name will be spoilt. At the same time some younger men are very clear about the fact that values have changed and that the elders are living with blinkers on. I have seen shifts in attitude; for example, the patriarch, male head of the family, appearing to be strict and unbending is different today in that his concern is about his daughter's well-being as opposed to maintaining her reputation so that she does not bring shame to her family and its standing in society. This probably is due to the smaller family unit living in close proximity and not as an extended family; relationships are much closer and less distant as they used to be in the old days.'

My participants drew out distinct gender differentiation shaping the expectations placed upon them. Women are expected to be well-mannered, submissive, social housewives. It was down to them to keep social circles and the family relationships maintained. Shanti remarked, 'When you are at the parents' house it is very strict. The women are relegated to the kitchen area. If men are in the front room, you are not allowed to sit there. I had to do all the chores before school and after school; it was split between me and my sisters. The boys did nothing and the rules are still the same here. You have to follow whatever the parents say.' Bhakti agrees that nowadays females are becoming equal and are offered the same chances, with a greater degree of freedom. She recalls how she couldn't go out as a couple in the past when she lived in India. It was not until she moved to Africa that she experienced such a liberty. That has all changed now – including women being allowed in the same room as men.

Shanti saw little change in her role as a woman in Britain to that of her existence in her homeland of India: 'Here the role is the same but more focused on immediate family, plus also having the responsibility of a job. You have to do everything from A to Z. The only difference is you had people in India to do certain chores for you.'

Krishna presented a distinct patriarchal dominance in her maternal household. 'My family [in Coventry], and I mean my nuclear family, is patriarchal. Things are done as Dad wants them done. This means that the rules in the house, morals that were instilled in us, were directed by my dad. Mum just had the job of enforcing those rules. Now the problem here, as I see it, occurs when Mum can be more forgiving and Dad won't be. There are things that Dad can't accept today, even though he has been here for forty years and can seem very liberal. For example, my dad wouldn't have been able to accept it if I had found my own life partner and wanted to marry him unless he was from our *samaj* [community]. The idea of having a relationship with somebody that wasn't Gujarati, or, God forbid, was white, black or Muslim (God forbid!) would have killed my Dad and certainly our relationship. Now if I had found somebody, I have no doubt that my dad would have disowned me but that my mum wouldn't have been able to keep contact with me either, even if she could have accepted it. As a result of this, I decided early on that there was no point in having a relationship with anybody unless I was prepared to lie through my teeth in order to have one, and to be perfectly honest, I was just too lazy to do that!'

Both Parisa and Krishna have seen a change in attitudes through the generations. Paradoxically, Krishna feels we are perhaps lagging behind India in our cultural thinking: 'All I can say is that the impression that I get is that everybody is far more forward in India than here. Their thinking is more Western than my thinking is. For example, in Kolva, in the eldest uncle's house, a widowed auntie has two bachelor sons and a son that is married. Now the daughter-in-law is able to live with the fact that she has a son from her first marriage that she never sees – no contact with him at all. She also had a house built for her separately so that she can live with her husband and son without the extended family. Now take me, who after your Bapa (Grandad) died, asked your Ba (Grandma) when she was coming to Leeds, as it would be better for her (and, selfishly, for me) if she was with us and we could keep an eye on her. It also allows your mum and her sister to live in relative peace as it means that they don't have to be concerned for her.'

Parisa explained that 'having lived a long time in proximity to the main society has meant that the new generation is much more anglicised, with values that are more placed in the British society, such as dating and marriage preferences being one's own choice as opposed to being arranged. Immersing into the cultural framework of music and media, values of life expectations, etc. have changed. Parents, too, are changing their views and expectations to more realistic ones of compromising with their children. There is still a little tension, and parents expect their daughters to make some realistic choices as the prejudices of their parents are challenged. So girls are still more closely monitored, although expectations are still the same for the males.'

The conversations and stories shared by the women I spent time with reveal the contradictions and ambiguities they articulated. They are quick to highlight the difficulties they face, agreeing that a system of male privilege underlies the value systems that restrict them. These assertions of male privilege are most acutely projected at the point of marriage. It should be noted here that the term 'arranged marriage' is often misinterpreted. In Indian cultures, the term 'arranged' means the parents often introduce their son or daughter to suitable life partners, and they – the children – do have their own say in whether or not they wish to commit. Commitment is required, and a couple should be engaged before they are permitted to date, although this has changed in recent times, with issues such as premarital sex raised in today's Western diaspora. If a Hindu Indian woman does not remain a virgin at the time of marriage, she is seen as 'second-hand'. Virgins still embody great prestige in British Indian society, and are chosen to partake in rituals prior to and during Hindu wedding ceremonies.

For Krishna and Parisa, their arranged marriages brought tension as they had to negotiate with their new family what their new role would be whilst trying to simultaneously retain the financial independence they enjoyed through their careers. They felt their secondary status was reaffirmed through practices such as dowry, which literally and symbolically reduced them to a commodity traded at the point of marriage. Their respect for the older generation, with the importance they too invested in their cultural heritage, limited the extent to which they challenged these practices, though it is clear they have caused anguish. Furthermore, my storytellers supported the arguments made by academics such as Leslie, whose work I summarised above, when they spoke of how Hindu epics such as the *Ramayana*, retold throughout their upbringing, promote marriage as central to a woman's role. The centrality of marriage in women's lives makes it difficult for a woman to choose not to marry and therefore escape dowry. The relationship between religion, patriarchy and dowry leaves women vulnerable to associated forms of violence. In Hindu tradition, the dowry serves as an economic transaction which symbolically suggests that the woman is a commodity, with the role to serve and work for the family. Shanti mentioned the direct impact of the dowry system on Hindu marriage: 'Women were treated as a piece of property. Economically, women relied on husbands for money as women didn't have jobs back then. The social position of the man was powerful, secured by holding power over the females. He gained prestige according to how much influence he held over them.'

Parisa reinforces the historical importance of dowry practice: 'Historically the system was introduced to prevent the larger portion of the wealth moving into another family, the dowry being a compromise. In the days when boys were looking after their parents, when money was tied up in large chunks of land, it made sense. Since wealth determines your position in society it made sense. Yet today this makes little sense in a country where the wealth is not tied up in land, where the welfare of the parents can be in the hands of a girl as well as the boy. Both girls and boys are now working, so gender division has changed; girls are able to pay towards their marriage ceremony in many cases so the parents are not spending a differentiated amount on them as opposed to their sons. So dowry has little place in this country; equal shares of their entire heritage is a fairer and just system for both sexes. By keeping the dowry system and buying into it we are subjecting ourselves to the strict rules of caste which impose expectations over what and how much should be given: the higher the caste, the greater the amount expected to be given. Certainly it is a costly process if there is more than one daughter involved. Furthermore, pressures build when expatriates return to India with their pounds which will buy a lot of dowry when converted to Indian rupees. Those of us left in the UK have to try to match the quantity of goods purchased during Indian weddings; here everything is so much more expensive so it is very difficult. Those of us who still aspire to a traditional Hindu life continue with dowry, but some now are choosing to bypass this ritual. Dowry only remains for those of us who still believe in the tradition of giving to our daughters, even if it seen as supporting her unequal status. Simply to fulfil a tradition is important to us because it is part of who we are, what makes us Hindu and *Brahmin*.'

Parisa continued that 'apparently, the dowry system even for us used to be that the girl's family and the boy's side would give jewellery to the bride. As times became hard the male side dropped this tradition and the bride no longer received jewellery from her future husband. Now that wealth has picked up, mainly because the employment opportunities for men and women have improved and families generally enjoy more wealth, this pratice has come back. Commonly, some sort of jewellery is now given when the bride first comes into her new marital home; she will bend down for blessings (*pagay lagay*) and receive her gifts: this is a sign that old values are being reasserted.'

Krishna recollects her marriage dowry: 'I have pictures of everybody sat down towards the end of my marriage, where my folks were giving gifts to everyone on our side of the family. It is a cultural obligation, almost: dowry is given in this country as invisibly as possible through the guise of marital gift-giving; it is not obvious that it is dowry given by the bride's family to the groom's, but this is what is going on. I had clearly said to my dad, when we talked about me getting married, that if he *had* to pay a dowry for me then I would break my relation with that man and the family. I am not an item in my family to be sold and that would go against myself-respect, especially as I have the capacity to earn in my own right. No dowry was asked for me; the "gifts" were from my mum and dad.

'As for the gifts, it is still a way to keep the girl's family on their toes. I know that whilst my mum and dad were giving gifts, they were asking for forgiveness: had any mistakes been made in the wedding ceremonies? You can imagine as a young twenty-two-year-old hothead that would have messed my head up! And it isn't just when you get married that that happens ... When my father-in-law died my husband was doing the *puja* on the twelfth day. The gifts that were given to everybody in the family after the *puja* was finished were from my mum and dad. The reason again was that they were asking for forgiveness in case the daughter they had brought up had not done her duty in looking after her father-in-law, in case somehow I might have been to blame. The money given was collected and then donated to charity. There is a cultural pressure on a girl's family to fork out for a lot of things, even in this day and age.'

The *mangalsutra* symbolises that Hindu women must remain conscious of their *dharma* (duty and rules). *Stridharma* specifically refers to the code of righteousness for women. Again, the origins of *dharma* lie in the religious scriptures. Gold is highly prized as a dowry because it is thought to symbolise Shakti, a reminder of women's energy and power which must be used for the purpose of raising a family. Stringed black beads are often worn during weddings and represent the Hindu God Shiva who symbolises fertility, further embedding this notion that the primary purpose of marriage is reproduction and the nurturing of children. Krishna discussed the importance of the *mangalsutra* (*mangal* means auspicious and *sutra* the thread) to her: 'The *mangalsutra* is our wedding chain and in it the black beads are significant. The signs of an Indian women being married are: *chandlo* (or *bindi*), which is the mark made from red powder on the bride's forehead which signifies Lakshmi, the goddess of prosperity – the symbol represents the hope that the the bride will bring prosperity and good fortune to her husband's family; *mangalsutra*, which is a pendant symbolising marriage usually made of gold; and bangles, also worn by the bride as a sign of her marital status. When you get married, that's what we gain. The *mangalsutra* has black beads to ward off the evil eye from the couple. It's been ingrained into my psyche that you can only wear it if you are married, so I made a decision when I got married that I would wear it. I don't believe in it warding off the evil eye but I do believe that I will wear it as long as my husband is around. As an Indian, now would be the time to say that if I was lucky, then I would die first and die as a *Sughaan* (married woman) so I don't have to go through the being widowed syndrome. As a Western woman, I want to say c'est la vie and what is going to happen is going to happen!'

The symbols women wear at the point of marriage act as visual reminders of their role but also link them to the domestic sphere, reminding them that it is their responsibility or *dharma* to maintain family well-being. If anything goes wrong within a family – if a child gets sick or a husband dies – blame is first directed towards the wife and mother who it is assumed has failed in some way. Denying women financial independence is key to ensuring that they remain subordinate and dependent on their fathers and husbands. Dowry functions to practically insure that women remain linked to their domestic role with few other options available. Indian women throughout history have challenged their subordinate status and the Indian feminist movement remains coherent and publically visible. Despite the existence and continuance of these traditional patriarchal values women do not passively accept them and my storytellers clearly demonstrate this through their views.

I believe, based on my experience and those of my peers, that Hindu women in the UK find it much harder to find spaces to express their personal feelings. In India many more private and public women-only spaces exist. For example, Bradley (2010) talks about how women-only ritual spaces are also social opportunities for women to share their troubles and joys. These kinds of women-only spaces do not exist in the same way here in the UK, where Hindu women are perhaps even more closely scrutinised by others in their community who fear they may be led stray by the evils of secularism.

My storytellers went into far greater depth than I anticipated; I ended by asking them if there was any aspect of their culture or role which they wished to change. Bhakti was quick to bring up issues of dowry practice. She did not view it as being morally just and felt women were being sold. But she observed that 'it is so deeply engrained in our culture, and linked into ideas about gender that are in turn promoted by our religion, how can we ever dismantle it?' After a pause she becomes more optimistic that 'dowry will die out very quickly as there are more and more inter-caste marriages taking place. The next generation will no longer value or pay attention to such things.'

Shanti acknowledged that 'it's difficult to make decisions for yourself. Females always have to compromise and that isn't fair. Even if you marry within the same caste there is still going to be a difference in opinion. Girls are still treated differently. Boys stay at home so there isn't that much pressure.' If Shanti could change any aspect of her gender role in India, she would grant equality, 'for everyone to be given the same opportunities; giving them an equal balance in life and responsibility. Also to develop everyone's self-worth and help everyone that is suffering.'

Parisa and Krishna shared similar wishes to rectify the social stratification within family structure. Parisa noted 'the need for equality in treatment, in all aspects of the societal life, from marriage to staying with the daughter, to heritage ... the fact that the boy's side of the family still has a precedence over the girl's and that their parents are treated less favourably than the male's and do not have equal rights to be involved in the female's life after she gets married. For my generation the inequality of treatment by our own parents, especially for me with my mother treating my brother more favourably than me, was something I disagree with. Not having equal rights to my heritage because I am a female and more so because I was my parents' career for such a long time is very hurtful.'

Krishna's added in conclusion: 'There are two things in our culture that I don't agree with. The first is that there is a hierarchy of professions and that teaching isn't anywhere near the top of that list. In my head, if it wasn't for the teaching profession, there wouldn't be your lawyers and accountants and your blessed doctors! I hate being looked down on because I don't conform to what Indians think is the ideal job! The second thing that I don't agree with is this culture of blaming the woman if something goes wrong in a marriage. If a divorce happens it will be the woman's fault, regardless of what the male did. Also (now that I am on a roll) the caring female in traditional extended families always seems to get shat upon! You know what I mean Charlenie!'

Conclusion

My storytellers have left me with little to say: their narratives have eloquently and sensitively revealed this complex web within which they live. They respect their culture and traditions yet also see with certainty the limitations it has brought upon them. They have faith that as the generations grow in number, practices that transmit the most blatant and oppressive values, such as dowry, will be eradicated. Herein, there is clearly a long way still to go and what these stories highlight is that migration to the UK has indeed opened doors but traditional values still prevail. Women are primarily left exposed to the continued expectations of their families to be the bearers and upholders of culture even when they also hold professional positions. Greater and wider acknowledgement of the struggles BME women face would be the start of more open discussions within communities and between different groups in wider society. This I hope would help women like me find an improved and organic balance between our aspirations for a new way of living and our traditional values and beliefs.

Notes

1 For more details about the Hindu caste system and campaigns to eradicate it see Kishwar, 1996, a, b, 2000.

2 *Puja* literally means 'honouring guests' and is a ritual performed to Hindu deities. Women are traditionally responsible for performing *puja* in the home and do so to ask the deities to protect their family.

7
The Big Taboo: Stories of Premarital Relationships

Sana Khilji

As with the previous chapters, the authors have chosen the topics covered because of their experiences or the stories they have heard from others within their diaspora community. The stories, despite their differences, contain common narratives that reflect at times the harsh realities of life as a woman across cultures, but also highlight the pride and importance of religious and cultural heritage as dimensions that give life purpose and direction and help women, despite the difficulties many face. In this chapter I present stories about women who have faced emotional challenges attempting to navigate between the expectations of their parents and the 'freedoms' they feel they have in the UK.

Although it is common to hear accounts of men and women who have entered relationships with people from outside the diaspora community it is generally frowned upon. As commonly reported, it represents a source of real tension between the older and younger generations. The older generations want to see their cultural heritage preserved through marital unions between those that share the same background. The younger generation is now mixing at school and outside with people from so many backgrounds that this opens up the possibilities for finding a partner from outside of their parent's approved group. These tensions culminate in a spectrum of outcomes from emotional and psychological stress to – as Chapter 8 covers – forced marriage and other cases of gender-based violence. Honour killings are at the very extreme end of this spectrum and although for many of the women I have spoken with they do not fear violence or death, they do recognise that this tragic end for many begins with the anger, shame and disappointment parents and grandparents express when confronted with premarital relationships. This disapproving reaction explains the extreme secrecy surrounding these relationships and the difficulty in quantifying just how many young men and women engage in them. This chapter is an attempt to offer some personal insights into how two young Muslim women from differing cultural backgrounds, Somali and Pakistani, respond to and navigate around the expectations of their parents and seek to fulfil their own personal desires to pursue relationships with men prior to marriage. These stories also challenge assumptions that all such relationships end in violence and that all Muslim parents are unreasonable and unwilling to support their children in finding their own partners. The chapter ends with an interview with one liberal-minded Muslim father. Although not in any way representative of all Muslim fathers in the UK, he talks openly about the change in attitude he has had to accept as a result of migrating to the UK. The shift in his view is a signal of hope that his liberal views may well prevail, reducing the number of instances of forced marriage and gender-based violence BME women endure as a result of misogynistic and strictly upheld views on relationships.

Elisha's story

Elisha is a twenty-three-year-old second-generation Somali woman. There isn't much more I can say about her, other than she is an elegant Muslim woman living an independent life in Britain, studying and working in order that she can secure a good future. She considers herself British and has many friends both inside and outside of her immediate diaspora. Some of these friendships have been with non-Somali men and have become particularly close.

The first such friendship Elisha speaks of is with a man named Baz. When they first met, he was nineteen, and she was fifteen. It began at her bus stop where she caught her bus to and from school each day. The first time they had met, they started talking; and then the second time he asked for her number. At the age of fifteen, her parents hadn't allowed her to have a mobile yet; so instead Baz gave his own number to her. She had to use her house phone to ring him. Gradually over time she began to trust him and look forward to their conversations. After a few weeks of telephone conversations they started to see each other more formally. Elisha spoke of how she would sneak out of school to meet him, as it was only during school that it was possible for her to meet him: 'I would leave during lunchtime, because year tens and elevens were allowed out for lunch. I would just not come back, and so basically bunk my afternoon classes. He would pick me up and would take me to Starbucks or somewhere like that.'

I asked Elisha why it was that during school hours was the only time she could see Baz, and she answered that her parents would not allow her to go out on her own after school, not even with her friends. The expectation was that she would leave the house only to go to school and would return immediately. She also said that she had not told anyone about this relationship, not even her friends; she was too afraid that it would get back to her parents. She then told me that she asked Baz always to drop her in time for her to get home at her usual time, so as not to raise any suspicion with her parents. Although she shared with me how badly she felt at lying to her parents, she also acknowledged that 'despite this I still wanted to see him'. I asked her what was so important about her relationship with Baz that meant she was prepared to lie to her parents. She spoke about how he listened to her, that she could talk, for the first time, about how she really felt about her life. He was mature and seemed to understand where she came from. Throughout this relationship she feared her father finding out: she knew as soon as he did he would not only make sure it ended but also prevent her from going to school. In the end Elisha realised that Baz wanted more from her than she was prepared to give and ended it.

Elisha even talked of being slightly relieved when it was over, now that she did not have to lie anymore. She said that her father's reaction would not just have been founded on his own concerns but also fears about how the community would react if they discovered that Elisha had been seeing a man in secret. Relationships between the sexes are only sanctioned during engagement or marriage; nothing outside of these arrangements are allowed. So tightly are relationships policed that even at the point of being engaged, the couple can 'only talk on the phone before marriage'. If a girl was found to have a boyfriend, rumours would spread like wildfire, and the girl (more than the boy) would be stigmatised forever. I asked Elisha, what kind of rumours? So she told me things like, 'she's Westernised', 'she's sleeping with a guy', 'her mum was like that', and other derogatory comments about her wider family. In other words, it would be assumed they were all bad, and shame would be brought on the whole family. Elisha went on that to 'be discovered with a boy outside of engagement, Somali or not, is taken as a sign of disrespect, and coming from a well respected family – it would tar them also'. Part of the reaction to relationships outside of marriage is justified and argued on religious grounds. Elisha stated that 'religion does not allow for a literal boyfriend'. She explained that as long as both 'families have spoken and agreed, it is only then that you can see him to get to know what he is like, but this is not tolerated for too long before an engagement is expected'. While marriage preparations are going on the couple may be permitted to speak within the company of others once in a while – but only for short periods of time.

Elisha's stopped for a while and then began again with another story of a relationship she had with a man called Hamud. Hamud was twenty-four years old, four to five years older than Elisha, who knew him through her family. He was in fact a far distant relative. Elisha was nineteen years old when she met Hamud. She elaborated that she knew Hamud beforehand; he had come round to her house and was well acquainted with the family. They started talking on the telephone every night – she had gotten permission for a mobile at the age of eighteen. Elsiha spoke of beginning to feel closer and closer to him. Through talking every night they built a connection even though they could only see each other once a month. Their meetings were restricted to college hours; the relationship had to be kept a secret even though Hamud was known to her family – their meetings outside of marriage would not have been sanctioned. Nonetheless, they enjoyed spending time together and felt close.

Elsiha talked again about feeling guilty; she felt she had let her parents down. In her own words she said she was 'betraying my parents, but I couldn't tell them this is what I'm doing'. Elisha felt unable to stop her meetings with Hamud; he made her happy so she continued to wrestle with her feelings of unease. When I asked Elisha what happened, she said one day, when she had gone to see Hamud, she 'looked into his phone, and saw messages I shouldn't see in my boyfriend's phone and after that I couldn't trust him. I felt like he was trying to hurt me.' When she confronted him, all he said was the texts were from 'friends only', but she didn't believe it, and 'couldn't take the lack of trust so called off the relationship'.

Elisha said how knocked she felt by this experience; Hamud had made her happy for a while and she had sacrificed her parents' trust for him. It took her a year to get through this break-up and during that time she still had to see him during family occasions. However, during this period Elisha met Ashfaq. He was also a relative from her step-mother's side of the family. At this point, she was twenty/twenty-one years old. Ashfaq's sister Heela was staying with her family as she had newly arrived in the UK. Elisha had responsibility for helping her settle into her new life in the UK. It was Heela who introduced Elisha and Ashfaq. Heela could not speak English and her brother, born in the UK, could not speak anything else. Heela asked Elisha to translate her emails for Ashfaq, and gradually he began to ask Elisha questions directly. Eventually they exchanged email addresses and began to communicate with each other directly.

A week or so later, they spoke on msn for the first time; Elisha wasn't usually allowed on msn, but stole an opportunity one day when she was alone in the house. Elisha and Ashfaq then started speaking on msn quite often, making it their main form of communication. A few weeks later – possibly two – he asked her out. The emails and phone calls carried on for four or five months, at which point Elisha said that she couldn't carry on any longer, and that Ashfaq needed to send his relatives for her hand in marriage. He agreed to this and called his sister as the only relative in the country and explained that he had grown close to Elisha and wanted to become engaged to her. He requested that Heela approach Elsiha's parents for her hand in marriage. Heela did not agree and told him directly that she would not approve the marriage. Ashfaq suddenly stopped all communication with Elisha, leaving her without an explanation for his silence.

Elisha's step-mother found out that there was something going on, triggered by her hearing a man's voice on the phone to Elisha. She immediately asked Elisha what was going on, at which point Elisha felt there was no point in hiding it any longer and came clean about the whole prolonged communication with Ashfaq. Elisha felt relieved that she was finally able to be honest and appreciated her step-mother listening to her without getting angry. They agreed not to tell her father who may not have reacted in the same calm manner. Elisha felt hurt and let down once more, firstly by Heela whom she felt she had built a close sister-like bond with, and then by Ashfaq who gave up so easily. He had not fought to marry her, and Elsiha could only conclude that she had never meant that much to him.

It had been about a year since Hamud had gone from her life, and then suddenly he returned out of the blue. At this point Elisha was in her last year at college, and was twenty-one years old. Hamud somehow managed to get her new number from her brother, and started calling continuously, saying that he still loved her and wanted to get back together, asking for another chance. Elisha didn't give in easily, but did eventually agree to see him – only, however, on the condition that he was willing to get married. She also stipulated that both their families must now know everything and he must promise never to go behind her back again. He agreed to this and formally asked for her hand in marriage.

The parents from both sides began to throw themselves into the wedding plans. Hamud and Elisha on the other hand were trying to work through some practical issues like should Elisha continue her studies, where would they live, etc? Elisha was in her final year of college and wanted to go on to university but Hamud seemed to have other ideas, and asked Elisha to 'hold off on the education', by which he meant he did not want her to attend university. Instead, he wished her to focus on starting a family. Elisha did not want this: she was determined to pursue her education at university and could not see why they needed to start a family straight away. She was also unhappy at the thought of Hamud's proposed living arrangements: he wanted them to move in with his sister as he didn't have parents and felt this was in fact their only option. Elisha wasn't fond of the idea of living with her sister-in-law and her babies; she wanted some privacy, which she would not get in that situation. Elisha confided in her step-mother and each time she received the same response: 'Just say okay so they don't feel uncomfortable.' Elisha felt as if Hamud was trying to control her; there were things she wanted for herself and she needed to make him understand.

For a while Hamud and Elisha did not speak, but gradually they began to work through their issues. Elisha simply told him that she was not happy with what he expected from her once married. She was clear she would feel extremely uncomfortable living with his sister, so he would need to find a house for the two of them. Hamud agreed to not living with his sister, but refused to be active in finding them a house. Elisha applied for and gained a place at university regardless of Hamud's feelings and they started looking for an apartment. However, more disagreements emerged. Hamud wanted to live in south London yet Elisha's family and her university was located in east London. She found this absurd, as she would have to travel for hours each day to get to university or to see her family. She also found Hamud's refusal to even look halfway between as a further sign of his selfishness. Elisha called Hamud and said that she couldn't take what he was doing, and that they needed to meet in the middle as a couple, and that she could not take his selfishness anymore. He simply said sorry, and that he would call her father and apologise, and explain that he was free to get her married elsewhere. Elsiha's father pushed them on to see whether they could resolve their differences but they both confirmed it was over.

Throughout all this experience Elsiha's parents were supportive, which gave her the confidence to push for what she wanted. One day Hamud's sister called Elisha's step-mother to find out what was happening; she said she was mad at him for the whole thing and wanted to try to fix things. But Elisha's step-mother just said that Elisha could not and would not be forced into marrying somebody that she did not want to marry. Then Hamud's brother-in-law called, and was extremely apologetic and ashamed and embarrassed at Hamud's behaviour; he kept saying that it was silly and again wanted to try fixing things. After this, Elisha's father called Hamud himself.

He got his number from Hamud's mother, who he himself knew as Elisha's step-mother's aunt. He felt the current situation was miserable for everybody, and as it was not making anybody happy, he felt it was worth giving it a shot in calling Hamud and seeing if he wanted to try work things out. Elisha's father tried to persuade him to speak to her, but Hamud replied with a blunt 'no'. Hamud went on to say that he didn't think Elisha wanted to speak to him or had any feelings for him so things should just be left.

Not too long after Hamud, Usamah came along. He was twenty-four; Elisha was twenty-one. He was introduced to Elisha's family through her uncles, who had brought him along during a family visit. During this visit Usamah had vaguely seen Elisha, but she had not seen him at all. Later, Elisha's uncle spoke to her father, saying that he thought the two should speak and get to know one another – which her father agreed to. The next day, Elisha's father told her that he had given her number to her uncle, who was in between the two families, to pass on to Usamah. A day later, he called, and they started speaking, and began to get to know one another over the phone. Elisha's uncle quickly said it was not good that two unmarried people were talking to one another so much, and that they should get the *nikkah* (Islamic marriage ceremony) done. Elisha's father agreed and her uncle went back and spoke to Usamah and his family to seek their agreement. The *nikkah* was done on 1 November 2008, with a bigger wedding following a few months later.

Farah's story

The second woman is a twenty-year-old named Farah. She's a strong-minded, liberally independent Pakistani Muslim. Her family encouraged her to be this way although still firmly observant of Muslim customs. The first man Farah met was Hannan, who at the time was seventeen years of age and in his first year of college. Farah at this point was also in her first year and was sixteen. They were both on the same IT course and so knew each other from class. About two months into college, Farah was walking out through the gates on her way home, where she went past Hannan who was smoking on the bench with his group of friends. He started following her, trying to get her attention; and just as she was about to cross the road called out her name. She didn't recognise him so carried on walking, but he ran up to her and started trying to make conversation, asking if she's new and where she was from. He told her he was from Leyton, and went to a boys school. She gradually realised that he was her cousin's best friend. When she mentioned this he explained that they weren't speaking any longer.

She had him drop her about a road away from her house – any closer would have been too risky as her family or others that knew her may have seen. She knew to be seen with him would cause tensions and arguments at home. When she was leaving, Hannan asked for her number, which Farah gave. A few days later she got a call from him; he wanted her to go out with him to dinner and clubbing. Farah had never gone out to such places or so late before, so she refused. Some days later, Farah realised this wasn't going to go anywhere. They had nothing in common, their timings were completely different and she simply didn't feel the same; so she ended the relationship about a week later.

The second man was Basil, who was nineteen at the time and in his second year at college. Farah was seventeen and also in her second year. They initially met during induction and were put into the same group. They sat at opposite ends from each other in their group. She felt his glare and tried to avoid looking at him. As part of induction the class were encouraged to exchange general information to get to know each other. Farah noticed that he kept smiling at her a lot – a kind of 'I like you' smile, as she described it to me. She told me that he went up to her and asked her the questions on the sheet and some extra details for his own benefit. They went back and sat down. He was sitting with his best friend, and she could feel his glare again and could hear them talking about her as well. She became quite uncomfortable at this.

About a week later classes started. On the very first day, Farah was on her way upstairs to her lesson, and Basil was waiting at the top of the staircase on his own, looking fairly lost. She acted like she didn't know who he was, and actually thought she had seen him elsewhere other than class and college, but wasn't sure. On the walk up to the classroom she found out that he only lived a road away from her. She told me she originally thought he was Turkish – 'he just didn't look Pakistani!' – but then found that he was half-Pakistani and half-white. Farah asked him why he was waiting at the top of the stairs, to which he replied he was waiting for his friend, not her. This led to a small playful argument, during which Basil admitted to waiting for her, hoping to catch her before class. They went in, and he walked to the back of the room, signalling for her to follow and sit with him.

They were on the phone the whole night after that, and told each other more about each other. The next morning, they both met an hour earlier than lessons, Basil took her into the building and out of the cold, and because it was so early it was still empty. They went down to the heater and just stayed there till it was time to go into class. It came to lunchtime, and as they walked to the front of the building, Basil's friends saw him, and asked to go to lunch. But he refused, so as to stay with Farah. They went to an empty classroom and just started talking. During this time, a friend named Dawar called. Basil got angry, feeling threatened by another man ringing, after which Farah and Basil did start to officially date.

A month into their relationship, Basil took Farah home to meet his mother, although she did not know this is what was going to happen – she thought the house would be empty. Farah asked about Basil's father, and he bluntly told her he was dead. They met and spoke more and more over time and went out during the weekdays. Farah's family were very strict about allowing her out with friends; she would sneak to places during the weekdays when they didn't know about it, but at the weekend it was impossible to do this. When I probed further into how she felt about hiding the relationship from her family, Farah admitted it was hard. She said that she felt bad for not telling them and lying about things, but she also knew she had to if she wanted the relationship to continue.

Farah ended the relationship with Basil after discovering he had cheated on her. It had lasted two years; she was nineteen by this point and he was twenty-one. After the break-up, Farah became really ill; she stopped eating properly and got taken into hospital for two weeks; her doctors put her on numerous medications in order to get her back to full health. All through this period Basil had also been calling; he was refusing to leave her be; but Farah had realised that it wasn't worth it – he had cheated on her twice by this point, and started wondering what else he may have lied about. So once she was discharged, she changed her number and focused on putting the past behind her. She did divulge how hard a process it was, and the emotions that made her feel as though she was incapable of getting on with somebody else.

Farah finally had started to feel freer at home feeling a weight of guilt had been lifted now she no longer had to hide a relationship from her parents. She then met Ehsan, who was twenty-three. The first time they met was at his workplace – which was a market stall he ran. Farah was out shopping with her cousin, and they spent about twenty minutes at his stall. She described herself as just standing there so he would start making conversation, and eventually he asked if she wanted some biscuits and they continued chatting.

Three months on, they bumped into each other again in a shop, which turned out to be his brother's shop. This time she was with her mum, but still made conversation with him – but just a general hello. Her mum was quite curious and enquired how she knew him. Farah replied that he used to live close to them, and so her mother greeted him too and made polite conversation. She then told her mum to go look at some other garment while she herself paid for what she wanted, but her mother refused to leave her side, giving her no opportunity to exchange numbers.

A week later, she was out with her friend deliberately trying to track Ehsan down. She did manage to bump into him and they finally exchanged numbers and began communicating via text straight away. He asked to see her the next day, but Farah refused, as she was expected at work. In quite a puzzled manner, she explained that he got a little angry at this and told her he didn't want to know her – which she still doesn't seem to understand. A week later he called again and acted completely normal, and on enquiry about his previous behaviour, laughed about it, saying he was only joking.

Farah and Ehsan now began to see each other regularly. About five months in, Farah met a few of his friends and co-workers as well, and told her own friends about Ehsan too. But another month into the relationship, and Ehsan having known that Farah was a virgin, wanted more of a commitment to him and asked for this. But Farah refused saying 'not before marriage'. This created more arguments and led to Ehsan accusing Farah of not being committed to the relationship and him if she didn't give him what he wanted. They continued dating for a month, but Ehsan made it clear that he would not marry Farah so there was no long-term future. Farah felt increasingly guilty that she was concealing yet another relationship from her parents, knowing that it would not lead anywhere. She knew her parents would put pressure on her to end this relationship. She confided that she did not know what to do; she enjoyed being with Ehsan but then felt guilty at home for not being honest. She talked about how she knew she was disrespecting her parents but somehow could not stop herself – she could not explain why, as she knew she would not marry this man. Despite these feelings Farah remained with him. They decided that they need not finish their relationship until they stop making each other happy.

A father's view

I felt it was important to try to gain some insight into these stories from a different perspective and asked a Muslim father of three daughters to share his views with me. Aarib is a well respected sixty-two-year-old man of the Muslim community in east London. He himself grew up in a rural area of Pakistan. Throughout his childhood his father would be away in the city for work and came home every so often when he was able to afford a break. He, with his brothers and sisters, worked their way up the ladder and eventually moved to the city, where he lived with his family till he migrated to the UK with his wife and two daughters. Having moved over on a temporary placement he made the decision to leave his job and remain in the UK. This decision was based upon the facilities and opportunities he hoped to provide for his children. He later had his third daughter, and about eleven years after that, he had a son.

I asked him how he would view any of his three daughters coming home with a man on their arm, or for himself and his wife to find one of them had a boyfriend. He explained, 'When I came to the UK I had to adjust my own upbringing and views to those of this new place in which I was raising my family.' He is fully aware of how premarital relationship is the norm in the UK but he wrestles with such behaviour which undermines so many of the traditional values that shape him.

He shared that he had adjusted to some extent. 'If you're living here and bringing up your kids in this environment then you need to accept these things happen. Some parents may feel like this is wrong, and have relatives to marry their kids to. But the kids also may like somebody and we have to accept this, as do the majority of people here now. It is rare to find this mindset. But there are limits too.' Asking him to elaborate on what he means by the 'limits' he became quite hesitant mainly because of my gender, He said that he 'will speak to me as he would his daughter, or any other girl asking him'. He then went on to define 'the line' as something physical which shouldn't be crossed, and something that if crossed at a young age 'is out of haste and lust, not thought upon'. I took from this that he felt the line was the point at which a relationship becomes anything other than a platonic friendship; in other words, girls can have friends who are boys but nothing more.

Aarib said that over the years he had relaxed and allowed his daughters to have boyfriends, trusting that they would not cross the line. He felt this period was an important build-up to marriage, emphasising that it is important for two individuals to get to know each other if they are going to spend their lives together. At the same time it is important for the parents and families to also approve. Marriage is an agreement between two families who sanction a union and so can't be left solely to the couple. 'But let me tell you, for instance: when we go into weddings, parties, dinners or any functions with our children, it does not matter if they are girls or boys. But having three girls, my wife and I know exactly which boys are looking at my daughters. As parents we know. We have our eyes on them and our children as well. We calculate everything and know what is going on. We know the families and we know what everybody is like as well. It does not matter if it's in a big hall or on the street or in the market, shopping – we always have our eyes on this.' He then laughed – knowing he had just disclosed information that being a parent he was aware any parent would know, but which no child would have realised. But like other parents living in the UK, having brought up their offspring in Britain, Aarib is more liberal than he may seem. He adds, 'If my children were to find someone for themselves I would like them to come to me then, when they are sure and serious that this is the person they want me to meet and judge for them against my criteria of a husband – as would most parents that hold the same or similar view.' This suggests that parents may know what is going on, but would not like to acknowledge it till their children are ready and willing to bring it openly to them in a mature manner, if at all. This gives more insight into why this is still such a taboo subject within the Muslim communities. He expressed as a parent his concern about finding out from others about their children having relationships. This would be troubling because other people in the community would have known before them. When I further inquired about this, Aarib revealed that he would be upset by the secrecy, the tar, possibly the age of the child, and mainly the stereotype of what happens in such relationships fogging the actuality of it all. He commented that 'only after a certain age would it be okay for boys and girls to start getting to know each other in a relationship. Not before.' He would rather his kids come to him about such things before anybody else did – as somebody else coming first would only inflict pain on himself and his family, making the matter worse.

The families have to feel confident that the match is right and that it will last. This is why daughters and sons should not necessarily be left to find their own partners. Aarib concluded, 'Obviously, being the father of girls I would like to satisfy myself and meet and get to know the boy. I would like to satisfy myself that he is good enough. If the boy is good enough and I am satisfied, I do not see why I would have a problem. I don't see why any parent would have a problem. We only want to see our children happy and successful in life.'

Conclusion

This last interview with a Muslim father cannot be taken as representative of all Muslim fathers and the chapter to follow highlights the consequences many girls experience as a result of breaking with the patriarchal traditions of their culture. However, it does challenge homogenous images of Muslim men as unreasonable, autocratic household heads. This interview does show that for some fathers their perceptions are changing as a result of living in the UK and although they still believe they have a central role to play in deciding who their children marry, they are willing to accept that their children may want to try to find a partner for themselves. The anguish shared by the daughter in the first story was proven in the end to be at least a little unnecessary given the level of concern her father later displayed and the support given to her by her mother. What I found from this last interview contradicts the view expressed by the second woman's story in which she felt she could not tell her parents about these relationships because they would not understand. Although premarital relationships are still a taboo subject in the Muslim community, there seems to be a wider agreement and acceptance that it should be allowed than my storytellers acknowledge. However, as the stories show, fear and anxiety about the reaction from parents is real and causes stress and tension.

8

'I Wish I'd Taken Her With Me': The Lives of Black and Minority Ethnic Women Facing Gender-Based Violence

Hannana Siddiqui

The last time I saw Banaz alive was in 2005 ... I wish with all my heart I had taken her with me in 2005 because she would then still be alive ... I find it really hard to say how much her death has affected me. Words just do not say enough ... I can honestly say there's not been one night without having nightmares. Banaz herself does not come into my dreams or nightmares, and that upsets me. I would like to see her again ... I cry and become very upset when I think what has happened to her. My life will never be the same again. (Bekhal Mahmod)[1]

This article follows the lives of three women from black and minority ethnic (BME) communities who have experienced gender-based violence, namely domestic violence, so called 'honour'-based violence, forced marriage and dowry abuse. It looks at the extremes as two cases resulted in murder or suicide, but it also examines women's experiences of routine abuse, which, if ignored, can escalate to tragedy. It places the lives of three women in the wider context of the BME women's movement and the gains and losses they have made in challenging violence against BME women. That context also includes a world where we witness a global recession and massive public sector cuts, a rise in religious fundamentalism and identity, the growth of the far right and 'rights for whites' demands, misguided social cohesion and anti-terror policies post-9/11 and a feminist women's movement fighting against violence against women and girls as one of its prime objectives. In particular, it looks at the work of a BME women's organisation, Southall Black Sisters (SBS),[2] which has led the way in raising and addressing these issues in relation to the needs of BME, particularly south Asian women, for over thirty years.

Sealed with a kiss

Banaz Mahmod, an Iraqi Kurdish woman, was only nineteen when she died. In April 2006 her body was found in a suitcase buried in the garden of an empty house in Birmingham – three months after being reported missing by her boyfriend, Rahmat Sulemani. Prior to her death, Banaz had reported threats to her life on four occasions, including an attempt on her life by her own father. She had even named the suspects who were later convicted of her murder. In 2007, her uncle, who is a powerful community leader, her father and a man from the Iraqi Kurdish community in south London were convicted of murder at the Old Bailey. Another two men were later also convicted of murder after being extradited from Iraq, where they had fled to escape justice.

Banaz had been murdered in a so called 'honour killing' for wanting to divorce her husband and to marry Rahmat. Her family did not approve of him as he was from another tribal group. Her uncle first made threats, and her mother warned her that her life was in danger, when Banaz had been seen kissing her boyfriend outside a Tube station. Her fate had been sealed with a kiss. However, her life, even prior to this, was full of abuse and torture. As a child she suffered at the hands of her strict father, as did her four sisters. Her brother, and other male relatives in the extended family, also policed her and her sisters' behaviour. Her older sister, Bekhal, had run away from home as a teenager. Bekhal reports experiences of physical violence, and pressure to conform to Islamic and Middle Eastern traditions and values, such as pressure to wear the veil and have a forced marriage. Later, Banaz was pressured into marriage, which led to separation. In July 2005, Banaz had accused her husband of domestic violence and rape, and had returned home to her parents in the hope that she would be able to obtain a divorce.

In the meantime, although in care and in hiding from her family, Bekhal had maintained contact with some of her siblings. On one occasion, she agreed to meet her brother. He had asked her to carry a suitcase for him and accompany him to a house which he had been instructed to clear for his father. He made Bekhal walk in front of him, and took her to a remote area where he attacked her. While walking behind, her brother had put on gloves and taken out a hammer. He hit her on the head with hammer, but when Bekhal fought back, he started to cry, saying that his father had told him to kill her. Although Bekhal had reported the incident to the police, it did not result in a prosecution.

This incident with Bekhal was a sinister forerunner of events which occurred in relation to Banaz. On New Year's Eve in 2005, Banaz had been asked by her father to bring a suitcase to her grandmother's house which he was clearing. While there, although very disapproving of alcohol, Banaz's father plied her with brandy to numb her resistance while he prepared to strangle her by putting on some gloves. However, when he attacked her, Banaz managed to struggle free and ran into the garden, where she tried to summon help by knocking on the neighbour's window. There was no response and she accidently broke the window. She eventually escaped by climbing over a garden fence to a cafe, bleeding and bare footed, where the police were called.

Banaz begged the police to call her boyfriend, Rahmat, who she felt was also in danger. On a previous occasion, there had been an attempt to kidnap him. He joined her at the hospital where Banaz was taken for treatment of her injuries. At the hospital, Banaz explained to the police that her father had attempted to kill her. The officer, however, was dismissive of her claims, treating her as if she was a 'melodramatic', attention-seeking drunk. Rahmat recorded Banaz's allegations on his mobile telephone, and believing that her mother would protect her from further harm, Banaz returned home. The police later considered charging Banaz for criminal damage for breaking the neighbour's window, but the case was discontinued when the neighbour did not pursue the matter.

At trial, Rahmat played Banaz's recorded message on this mobile telephone. It was a poignant moment, repeated many times as the message was relayed on television. The plot to kill Banaz had been hatched after a 'council of war' meeting organised by the uncle, who recruited three men to carry out the murder. On the morning of 24 January 2006, these men tortured, raped and sexually assaulted Banaz for about two hours before strangling her with a bootlace at her parent's home. Her body was then bundled into a suitcase. These men, who were secretly recorded in prison while awaiting trial, laughed and joked about what they did to Banaz. They said they kicked and stamped on her neck 'to get the soul out' and raped her 'to show her disrespect'. They also described how the uncle help drag her body in the suitcase from her home to a waiting car. One of them said, amid laughter, 'The road was crowded and a police car came by. Cars were passing by and we were dragging the bag. The handle broke off. Man, I swear I was standing there, I almost ran away ... her hair was sticking out, her elbow was sticking out. It was a stupid, silly thing. We put the bag on our shoulder to take it away.'[3]

SBS helped Banaz's sister, Bekhal, to give evidence for the prosecution. She did this at great risk to herself and is now on a witness protection scheme. Bekhal had been devastated by the death of Banaz, and dismayed and angry about the failures of the police to protect her. Unfortunately, an investigation into the case by the Independent Police Complaints Commission resulted only in 'words of advice' – minor disciplinary action – against some of the police officers to whom Banaz had turned to save her life.

Death at Southall railway station

'Harjinder' was a twenty-seven-year-old Asian woman born in the UK. She met her future husband in India and married in 1996. Harjinder's first child was a girl; because the family had expected a first born son, she felt she had let them down. Her domineering mother-in-law criticised her cooking and housekeeping.

In 2004, having reported assault to the police, her husband was issued with a formal caution. He left her and returned to India, threatening divorce. Her in-laws and relatives accused Harjinder of bringing shame and dishonour on the family as a result of the separation. A reconciliation was effected and the husband returned home on the condition that he would not do any domestic chores and she would not call the police again. Her husband neglected his responsibilities, and Harjinder struggled to cope on her own.

Harjinder became overly anxious that she was not caring for the children properly, although there was no evidence to suggest that this was the case. Her GP diagnosed depressive illness of moderate severity, which became more acute in a crisis. She admitted contemplating suicide and self-harm to the doctor during 2004, particularly when her husband left, even though she said that because of the children, she had no intention of killing herself. After their reconciliation, she told medical staff that the situation at home was worse than ever and regretted going to India to reunite with her husband. At various times, she told staff that she did not want to bring up the children on her own as her mother had done.

In August 2005, Harjinder jumped in front of a train with her two children at Southall railway station. Six months later, Harjinder's mother also jumped under a train on the same spot. The mother's suicide note said that she could not bear to be without her children and had been in receipt of bereavement counselling and anti-depressant medication.

At the inquest into the deaths, the coroner returned a verdict of suicide for both women, and unlawful killing by Harjinder of the children, brought on by depression and mental health problems. In an expert report to the coroner, SBS highlighted the relationship between depressive illness, domestic abuse and cultural pressures, which the coroner failed to take into account. SBS said:

[Harjinder] was diagnosed as suffering from a depressive illness of moderate severity, which became more acute in a crisis. She had contemplated suicide previously, particularly during times of marital strife and abuse.

Although this illness is an important factor in determining the reasons for [Harjinder's] and her children's deaths, [Harjinder's] depression is likely to have been compounded by violence, neglect and lack of support from her husband, who used the threat of divorce to enforce a reconciliation on his terms and conditions, which included him not doing any domestic work and [Harjinder] not making any more reports of violence to the police. This would have deterred [Harjinder] from making any further reports of abuse to the police or any other agency, and even to relatives and friends.

In 2005, near the time of her death, [Harjinder] had indicated her regret at having gone to India and that the situation at home was worse than ever, suggesting that her husband may have become more abusive and/or even less supportive. It appears that [Harjinder] still feared the possibility of divorce or separation if she challenged her husband's behaviour and having to bring up her children as a single parent. Her fears of hardship and social stigma and castigation supported by religious and cultural notions of shame and family honour which confine women to a pariah status would have been based on her childhood experiences of her mother's divorce and struggle as a lone parent.

It is likely that she would have feared a similar future for her children, who would have been twice affected by social disgrace through their mother and grandmother. In particular, it would have lowered the marriage prospect of her daughter. Although it is rare for women to take the life of their children, it is also possible that [Harjinder] feared that her husband would have neglected or not taken proper care of the children if she was no longer around to look after them.

Die at home rather than leave

After marriage in India, 'Gurpreet' came to join her husband in Britain. She experienced abuse from her husband and her mother-in-law. She experienced harassment from them for not bringing in enough dowry. Forced to sell her jewellery to pay the dowry, she was imprisoned in the house where her husband would frequently rape her. Her sister-in-law would also beat her and encourage others to do so. However, she was reluctant to leave because of the dishonour it would bring on her family. She was also fearful of being deported as she had entered the UK as a spouse. However, after a brutal beating, she was thrown out of the house. Her husband falsely told the police she was having an affair and had stolen from the family; the police took no action.

As she could not claim benefits because of her immigration status, Gurpreet was sent to live with another family member, who exploited her and made her cook and clean for the whole extended family, until she suffered injury and complained to her GP. Gurpreet became extremely depressed, developed an eating disorder, had trouble sleeping and suffered from anxiety attacks. In desperation, she approached the local temple for help, but they refused to assist her because of the shame she had brought to her family. Her imprisonment, isolation and language barriers meant that Gurpreet was unaware of sources of outside help. She was also denied help from her family overseas:

> My parents told me that I had to go back and make the marriage work. They were worried about how this would be seen in the community, and how they would be dishonoured by my very presence ... some people in the community put pressure on me to reconcile with my husband so that I would not continue to bring dishonour. When I have to tell people that I am divorced, no one asks why. They simply assume that I must have been wrong, that it was my fault. They want me to die at home with my husband rather than leave him.[4]

Gurpreet's GP prescribed anti-depressants, and referred her to SBS, whose psychotherapist diagnosed post-traumatic stress disorder. Gurpreet felt that SBS helped to empower her and regain a sense of self-worth. She developed a strong support network, a sense of independence, and eventually with the assistance of SBS obtained indefinite leave to remain in the UK.

No options – pressures inside and outside the BME community

The lives of these women show the complexities and pressures experienced by BME women experiencing domestic violence and harmful traditional practices. Research shows that south Asian women are up to three times more likely to commit suicide than women in the general population (Raleigh, 1996),[5] and have a disproportionate rate of suicide ideation and self-harm (Bhugra et al., 1999).[6] There is also some evidence to suggest that migrant and BME women have a disproportionate rate of domestic homicide (Mayor of London, 2010),[7] and that the Metropolitan Police have identified an average of twelve cases of 'honour' killings per year,[8] which predominately involve cases of south Asian and Middle Eastern women. SBS have found similar trends in its work. Over thirty years, it has dealt with eighteen cases of suicide (or death by unknown causes)[9] and at least ten cases of homicide.

We often ask ourselves why women feel they have no option but to kill themselves. Equally concerning is why they remain in abusive situations until they are murdered. Research shows that Asian and other BME women take longer to leave domestic violence (Thiara and Roy, 2010),[10] which inevitably leads to escalating abuse. Experience shows that BME women are subject to additional barriers to escaping abuse which exist both within and outside the community, which accounts for the disproportionate rate of suicide and self-harm, and domestic homicide, amongst this group.

Cultural and religious values and norms within minority communities reinforce patriarchal power structures and conservative social expectations of women. Notions such as 'shame' and 'honour', for example, are prevalent is south Asian and Middle Eastern communities, which require women to conform to traditional prescribed gender roles as dutiful and obedient wives, mothers, daughters, sisters and sisters-in-law. They are expected to suffer domestic violence in silence, and save their marriages or stay at home with their parents prior to marriage at all costs in order to preserve the 'honour' of the extended family and the wider community. Women who transgress are regarded as having brought shame and dishonour, and can face severe 'punishment' or consequences. This ranges from being disowned and treated as a social outcast, to sexual harassment, assaults, attempted murder and murder in what are also called 'honour killings', as illustrated by the case of Banaz Mahmod. Others are driven to suicide and self-harm, as highlighted by the death of Harjinder.

In addition, many women come under pressure to reconcile with abusive partners or family members if they do leave home or challenge abuse. Informal mediation is often performed by family elders or community and religious leaders, who place women under pressure to attend large family and community meetings in order to reconcile the couple or family members. Women, who are often alone and powerless, are made to feel guilty for acting against cultural and religious expectations, and pressured into returning home. The violent behaviour often remains unquestioned, and even where promises are made by perpetrators to stop the abuse, these are soon broken with no sanctions by the family or community.

The growth of fundamentalism in all religions has added to this pressure on women within BME communities to conform. Young men in particular have taken on strong religious identities which reinforce conservative value systems. These men are becoming more organised in policing women's behaviour. This is seen in the growth of 'bounty hunters' or networks and gangs of men, particularly in the North and Midlands of England, tracking down Asian women who have left home and forcing them to return, or harassing them if they refuse. The experience of 'Jack' and 'Zena Briggs', a white/British man and south Asian woman, who have been 'on the run' for many years, is a case in point. They have been forced to change their identities to protect themselves from Zena's relatives, who wanted her to marry a cousin. These relatives have attempted to use 'bounty hunters'/private detectives and other networks to find the couple. The community have also become more organised by attempting to divert women into religious arbitration or *Shariah* courts, or faith-based organisations, including religious women's groups, offering mediation and reconciliation as a preferred alternative to using the criminal and civil justice systems to deal with domestic violence and forced marriage.

These pressures within the community are compounded by barriers to escaping abuse outside the community. Like Gurpreet, many women have an insecure immigration status – and face a stark choice: domestic violence or deportation. Many also have no recourse to public funds: women with immigration problems are not entitled to benefits or public housing, and are therefore economically dependent on violent partners or family members. They face another stark choice: domestic violence or destitution. The fear of deportation and destitution prevents many BME women from leaving, or forces them to return to, abusive situations. Indeed, in some cases, it has led to suicide. For instance, in one case handled by SBS, an Asian woman committed suicide after her abusive husband failed to regularise her immigration status.[11]

Poverty is also a key barrier to many BME women who often have low incomes as they are on benefits or concentrated in part-time work with low pay and poor conditions.[12] Homelessness or lack of decent housing can also cause them to return home. Pressures of being lone parents add to children's demands to return to home or see their father, who may use child contact to harass the mother or pressure her to reconcile. Racial isolation, particularly as many women end up on council estates with high rates of racial harassment, or institutionalised racism such as the failure to provide interpretation services, specialist provision or public housing and benefits for those with an insecure immigration status, may drive others back. Lack of knowledge of English and awareness of their rights or where to obtain help may also prove a barrier. Agencies may also turn women away in the name of 'cultural or religious sensitivity' – a form of racial discrimination as it ignores the needs of women within BME communities. This may have been the reason why Banaz Mahmod was not provided with assistance and protection by the police, particularly by the officer who was 'dismissive' of Banaz's allegation of her father's attempt on her life.

The BME women's movement: breaking the silence and demanding accountability

In 1979, when Southall Black Sisters first formed, it sought to challenge the intersectional discrimination based on race and gender experienced by BME women. SBS was also part of a wider BME women's movement which, until then, had tended to focus on addressing racism. Although SBS was born out of the anti-racist movement, its feminist strand emerged in the 1980s. Early campaigns included protesting against virginity testing at Heathrow airport[13] and the death of Asian women who were murdered or committed suicide as a result of domestic violence. Krishna Sharma, for instance, killed herself in 1984 after experiencing years of domestic violence from her husband. In response, SBS organised survivors to demonstrate through Southall and outside of the husband's house. This direct action aimed to name and shame perpetrators, a concept borrowed from the Indian women's movement. It was one of the first campaigns to break the silence on domestic violence within Asian communities in the UK. While BME women demanded accountability from the community, both conservative and progressive anti-racist community leaders attempted to silence them. SBS were accused of being an 'outside, Western force' and therefore not a legitimate voice within the community, while others accused them of 'washing our dirty linen in public' and thus undermining the anti-racist struggle.

While the 1980s was largely about raising the issue of domestic violence within BME, particularly south Asian communities, the 1990s was more about demanding protection and accountability from the state as epitomised by the celebrated case of Kiranjit Ahluwalia, an Asian woman who was convicted of the murder of her violent husband. In 1992, SBS successfully helped Kiranjit to appeal against conviction, which was reduced to manslaughter, and she was released from life imprisonment. The case reformed the homicide law of provocation to take account of the 'slow burn' effect of domestic violence on battered women who kill, and propelled the issue of domestic violence within Asian communities onto the national agenda. However, more controversial cases, such as that of Zoora Shah, a working class non-literate Asian woman who killed a man with whom she had a long-term relationship, and who had sexually and economically abused and exploited her, forcing her into prostitution, was less successful. In 1998, her appeal against conviction for murder was refused on the grounds that her story was 'beyond belief'. The courts, it seems, still had problems in believing in Asian women's experiences of prostitution and sexual slavery. Nevertheless, SBS later successfully reduced her twenty-year tariff to twelve years, and in 2006, Zoora was finally released on parole.

The case of Zoora Shah also indicated a wider problem that SBS experienced in routine cases of gender-based violence. The politics of multiculturalism demand that the state does not interfere within BME communities in order to respect cultural deference and maintain good race relations. This assumes that BME communities are homogenous with no power divisions. Indeed, it is assumed that self-appointed male conservative community and religious leaders, who act as the 'gatekeepers', represent the interests of the community to the state. However, this approach has undermined the rights of BME women and other subgroups because their needs are often ignored by these leaders, who seek to maintain the status quo rather than empower women or other vulnerable groups within BME communities. SBS argued that as minority communities were regarded as being self-governing, they were also assumed to be self-policing on issues such as domestic violence and forced marriage. This meant that the problem was often ignored by the community and the state, which colluded in the practice of non-intervention, mediation and reconciliation in the name of 'cultural sensitivity' and a fear of being labelled racist.

Mature multiculturalism and 'moral blindness'

However, in 1999, Mike O'Brien, the then Home Office Minister, supported the SBS demand for state protection when he developed the notion of 'mature multiculturalism' and said, in relation to forced marriage, that: 'Multi-cultural sensitivity is no excuse for moral blindness.'[14]

The trigger for this shift in the state's response to minority women began with the death of Rukhsana Naz in 1998, which drew widespread media attention to the problem of forced marriage. Rukhsana Naz was killed by her mother and brother for refusing to stay in a forced marriage and for becoming pregnant by her lover. They were convicted of her murder in 1999. At the same time the case of 'Jack and Zena Briggs' received widespread attention. These cases prompted Mike O'Brien to establish the Home Office Working Group on Forced Marriage. However, some members of the Working Group, including representatives of religious women's organisations, did not share O'Brien's vision of a 'mature multiculturalism'. They argued instead for a 'softer' approach to forced marriage. Their view was that the main focus should be on changing social and cultural attitudes through public education led by community and religious leaders. They also advocated that mediation between the victim and her family as a means of tackling forced marriage was a legitimate option. SBS opposed this position, stating that mediation was a dangerous practice because it placed victims under pressure to reconcile with family members without any redress to immediate protection and because it did not ultimately challenge the practice of forced marriage. SBS pointed to the case of Vandana Patel, an abused Asian woman, who in 1991 had been stabbed to death by her husband at a mediation meeting organised by the police at the Domestic Violence Unit at Stoke Newington Police Station. The police facilitated the meeting on the grounds that in domestic violence cases, it is 'legitimate for a couple to talk through their difficulties'.

The acceptance of mediation as a means of tackling forced marriage compelled SBS to resign from the Working Group, but not before they had successfully included the recognition in the final report, *A Choice by Right* (Home Office, 2000), that forced marriage is an abuse of human rights. SBS was later able to ensure that the guidelines on forced marriage issued by the Foreign and Commonwealth Office Community Liaison Unit (later to become the joint Home Office and Foreign Office Forced Marriage Unit) did not recommend mediation as best practice. Following the Working Group's report, sustained pressure from SBS and others has led to an improved response from the Forced Marriage Unit, particularly to those cases of forced marriage that have an overseas dimension. However, implementing and enforcing the guidelines to prevent an indifferent or cultural relativist approach, by agencies such as the police and social services, has proved more difficult. However, SBS supported the creation of the Forced Marriage (Civil Protection) Act 2007 initiated by Lord Lester, which placed the forced marriage guidelines on a statutory footing.

Similarity and difference

These developments also highlighted some divisions or differences within the BME women's movement. While religious women's organisations favoured practices such as education and mediation, others, who argued for greater state intervention, were at times divided over strategy, such as differences between women's groups on the issue of so called 'honour' killings and 'honour'-based violence (HBV). In

2002, Heshu Yonis, a sixteen-year-old Iraqi Kurd, was murdered by her father for having a Christian Lebanese boyfriend, a case the media, for the first time in the UK, widely reported as an 'honour killing'. The division rested on how to conceptualise and therefore address HBV. South Asian women's groups like SBS, which have organised in the UK for over three decades, differed with the Middle Eastern women's groups, which represented more recent migrant communities. The Middle Eastern groups wanted to set the issue of HBV outside of the remit of domestic violence in order not to lose focus. They also argued that HBV is different from domestic violence because it involved the collusion of and harassment from the wider community. However, for SBS, the involvement of the extended family and the wider community has always been the dynamic of domestic violence within minority communities. Also, in most cases, HBV occurs within the context of or on the instigation of the family. SBS also argued that to include HBV as a cross-cutting issue on violence against women and girls (VAWG) does not dilute its significance, but rather ensures that black and minority women benefit from the progressive developments that have taken place on domestic violence and other forms of VAWG. In most cases, however, these differences have only been in emphasis, and Asian and Middle Eastern women's groups have often united to fight both domestic violence and HBV. For example, SBS worked together with a number of Middle Eastern women's groups to hold a memorial for Heshu Yonis under the common slogan of 'There is no "honour" in domestic violence, only shame!' SBS later also held a memorial for Banaz Mahmod.

Divisions over domestic violence are also reflected in the state's response to HBV. For example, while some within the police and the Crown Prosecution Service (CPS) wanted to locate HBV within the VAWG and domestic violence framework, others insisted that it was 'different' and therefore regarded 'culture' or 'race' as the basis of abuse experienced against black and minority women. This 'eroticisation' ignored the common underlying patriarchal power relations, and cultural and religious values systems, such as women being regarded as the property of men, which also justify VAWG in the wider society. The fact that many white men successfully plead provocation is similar to BME men making 'cultural defences' when killing women in the name of honour – both are arguing they killed because the woman did not fit the stereotype of the submissive faithful and obedient wife, daughter or girlfriend. So while we may argue that 'murder is murder', the tendency for wider society to view violence against BME women through the lens of HBV, ignores the role of patriarchy in the oppression of BME women.

Professionals also become confused about or ignore their responsibilities to tackle violence against BME women if they feel that HBV is something they do not understand or should not interfere with as a cultural and religious practice, or alternatively, are overzealous in their intervention because it is based on racial stereotypes. In the case of Heshu Yonis, the trial judge wanted to reduce the tariff on the grounds that it was a murder committed in the name of honour. This problem was also evident in the case of Harjinder. In 2010, an independent inquiry into her death overemphasised HBV in communities with 'honour systems',[15] to the detriment of acknowledging the issue of domestic violence suffered by Harjinder, and how this key matter concerning her safety – a routine issue for vulnerable adults which required standard procedures for protection to be implemented – was not handled appropriately by the mental health team. This included the need to refer Harjinder to a specialist BME women's organisation like SBS, which, in turn, would have also helped to reduce cultural and religious pressures on her. The implementation of standard procedures for protecting victims of domestic violence by the police may also have saved Banaz Mahmod's life.

The need to tackle both race and gender issues, however, is clear. Although there are major similarities between the experiences of abuse of white and BME women, there are also some major differences, which require specialist intervention and additional resources to tackle effectively. The disproportionate rate of domestic homicide against black and minority women has only recently been acknowledged and addressed, albeit in the context of 'honour killings' rather than violence against black and minority women more generally. Following a review by the Metropolitan Police in the early 2000s, which identified an average of twelve honour killings per year, we have witnessed a high conviction rate across the country in several high-profile so-called 'honour killing' cases. In some of these cases SBS played a role in helping to engage with the legal system, such as those of Rukhsana Naz, Heshu Yonis, Banaz Mahmod and Surjit Athwal.[16] This in itself is an indication of discrimination and the failure of the police, the CPS and the judiciary to tackle the problem in the past. However, this does not mean that routine cases of domestic violence/HBV, which form the majority, are effectively addressed. Neither does this deal with the other equally tragic, and more frequent, problem of suicide. While, in 2006, the CPS unsuccessfully attempted to prosecute a husband for driving his wife to suicide in the case of Gurjit Dhaliwal,[17] the government has done little to highlight this issue or make more resources available to remedy it. Similarly, the coroner's courts, which can make recommendations to agencies to prevent future fatalities, refuse to use these powers in cases of suicide driven by domestic violence and oppressive practices within the family. This happened in the case of Harjinder, despite expert evidence from SBS making the connection between abuse and her suicide. In another case, in 2002, SBS was forced to legally challenge a coroner's decision not to hold an inquest following the death of Nazia Bi, who died in a house fire in 1999 with her young daughter after informing the police that she was leaving her husband due to domestic violence. Although there was an attempt to prosecute the husband for murder, the case was dismissed following non-admission of crucial evidence by the trial judge. SBS called for an inquest when her family, who were related to the husband through a 'cousin' marriage, refused to do so. The coroner also refused to hold it, despite the violent unnatural death. It appeared that the coroner felt it was too 'culturally sensitive' to do so. Although the legal challenge was unsuccessful, the administration courts accepted that SBS would have been able to call for an inquest as an interested third party had they known Nazia Bi prior to her death.

Racism, religion and social cohesion

While there has been increasing recognition of the impact of multicultural politics in denying BME women access to state protection and accountability, the ugly head of racism and facism have also risen, particularly post-9/11, following which social cohesion policies have been more vigorously pursued. Although justified in the name of tackling terrorism and aiding integration, particularly in relation to Muslims, the call to adopt core 'British values' has blamed minority communities for extremism, and led to the demands for more 'rights for whites' by moderates and the growing far right movement, such as the British National Party and the English Defence League. Immigration controls, for instance, have also been justified in the name of social cohesion, and also, ironically, in order to tackle violence against BME women, particularly forced marriage. The government has argued that limits and conditions on migration should be imposed so that BME communities are encouraged to marry spouses from within the UK to enable greater compatibility, and erode 'backward' cultural values from overseas which justify forced marriage. In 2003, for instance, they introduced an age limit of eighteen for an overseas spouse entering the UK, which was later increased to twenty-one. While these measures are supported by some Asian women's groups, SBS and others opposed them because they divided migrant families in genuine marriages, and did little to protect victims of forced marriage, who face increased, not less, surveillance and control over their lives to ensure they sponsor their spouse into the UK. In 2010, SBS successfully intervened in two legal cases which challenged this policy, although this is a subject of further appeal by the Home Office.[18]

Social cohesion has also been used by racists to argue for diverting resources away from minority communities. In 2008, SBS successfully legally challenged the London borough of Ealing for attempting to withdraw its funding for specialist domestic violence services for BME women in the borough on the grounds that social cohesion policies forbade single group funding and on the assumption that race inequality no longer exists.[19] While this small yet ground-breaking victory has highlighted the need to provide specialist services for BME women experiencing abuse in the face of multiple barriers, the wider trend has been the mass closure of, or drastically reduced, services for BME women's organisations as result of funding cuts.[20] This has occurred for a number of reasons, including historical underfunding, the recession and cuts in public spending, and misguided social cohesion and assimilationist policies, resulting in money being diverted from specialist services to cheaper generic services provided by larger, even corporate, organisations, such as, for example, housing associations taking over Asian women's refuges.

Furthermore, and somewhat contradictory, state money has been diverted to faith-based organisations and initiatives under the 'Preventing Violent Extremism Fund' and the 'multi-faith' approach, which has, for instance, allowed state support for religious single sex schools, in a context where growing religious fundamentalism or stronger conservative religious identities flourish within BME communities. This has not only increased pressure on BME women to conform to traditional roles in the family, but has also led to a loss of secular spaces, including reduced funding for secular, feminist progressive BME women's organisations which challenge cultural and religious values and practices which oppress women. Due to the criticism of multiculturalism as a breeding ground for segregation and extremism, most recently articulated by David Cameron,[21] religion has now moved into the space occupied by culture. Under multi-faithism, violence against BME women is ignored due to the need for 'religious sensitivity'. According to the Muslim Arbitration Tribunal, the use of religious arbitration, for example, for domestic violence and forced marriage cases are accommodated by the state through the Arbitration Act 1996, as rulings by Sharia Councils can be upheld through the civil courts. [22]

Gains and losses

Despite these developments, and as a result of a growing momentum created by the BME women's movement, SBS have made some major gains. These have not only been in the field of forced marriage and HBV, but also legal reform and action plans on female genital mutilation and even some immigration issues. In 1999 SBS won a concession (later to become part of the immigration rules) which allowed overseas spouses subject to a probationary period to remain in the country permanently if they are victims of domestic violence. In addition, despite nearly twenty years of resistance by successive governments afraid of 'opening the floodgates' to migrants demanding rights to public housing and social security benefits, SBS have led a campaign which, in 2009, created a Home Office-funded pilot project to provide housing and financial support for women experiencing domestic violence and with no recourse to public funds. Indeed, the campaign has been so successful that the new coalition government has even committed itself to developing a long-term solution to the problem, which involves paying benefits for victims of domestic violence. The success of this campaign rests on our persistent efforts to expose the differential treatment experienced by migrant women when compared to those from the majority community, who have the safety net of being able to access state-funded housing and subsistence. The campaign has been fought in the context of demanding rights for all victims of domestic violence, where the government has a more progressive approach than that on race and immigration.

Our ability to hold onto these gains, however, is threatened by the demise of BME women's organisations. Major cuts in jobs, benefits and public spending also place greater pressure on BME women, who face the brunt of poverty. Their access to justice, services and resources is thus reduced, and their independence and empowerment severely hampered. The coalition government's 'Big Society' and localism agenda promises little to BME women, whose lives at the local level is constrained by a powerful male community and religious leaders, and where violence-against-women issues have no priority, or are handled internally through so-called 'education', mediation, reconciliation and religious arbitration rather than state intervention and protection. The move towards a greater use of restorative justice rather than other criminal justice penalties and mediation in civil litigation, particularly at a time when legal aid is being drastically cut, is an indicator of the state's collusion in these conservative local community agendas which aim to keep the family together without challenging abuse and the oppression of women.

Moving forward together

The lives of BME women have now reached a crossroads, or intersection, which leads in two directions: sexual oppression under greater pressures to conform to traditional gender roles; or an opportunity to determine their own destiny. The rise of religious fundamentalism and conservative religious identities within communities, and the collusion of the state under multi-faithism, have set back the struggle to hold communities and the state accountable for BME women's rights. Equally, this accountability is undermined by the growth of racism, nurtured by anti-terror-driven social cohesion policies in a context of a global recession and massive cuts in services, particularly those provided by secular, feminist and progressive BME women's organisations. The 'Big Society' agenda offers little in terms of real empowerment. However, BME women's fate is not fixed, and it is possible for them to gain their freedom through united action and strong alliances amongst feminists and other progressive movements. This means acting together to enable BME women to lead their own struggle so that they can win human rights for all. By so doing, they can respond to the regrets expressed by Bekhal Mahmod by saying that they will take women like Banaz, Hajinder and Gurpreet with them on their road to freedom, equality and justice.

Notes

1   The words of Bekhal Mahmod on the murder of her sister, Banaz Mahmod, quoted in Karen McVeigh, 'I wish I'd taken her with me', *The Guardian*, 21 July 2007.

2   Southall Black Sisters was founded in 1979 to address the needs of Asian and African-Caribbean women. It provides advice and advocacy services, and campaigns and conducts policy work on gender-based violence in minority communities, particularly south Asian. Although locally based, the work of SBS has a national reach due to its work on domestic violence and harmful traditional practices such as forced marriage, dowry abuse and honour crimes, and related issues of racism, poverty, homelessness, suicide and self-harm and immigration matters. Over the years, SBS has led the way in reforming the criminal justice system in relation to abused women who kill as illustrated by the high-profile case of Kiranjit

Ahluwalia. It has also been at the forefront of reforming immigration and the 'no recourse to public funds' law for women who experience domestic violence and have an insecure immigration status.

3   Karen McVeigh, '"Honour" killer boasted of stamping on woman's neck', *The Guardian*, 20 July 2007.

4   H. Siddiqui and P. Patel, *Safe and Sane: A Model of Intervention on Domestic Violence and Mental Health, Suicide and Self-harm Amongst Black and Minority Ethnic Women*, Southall Black Sisters Trust, 2010.

5   V. S. Raleigh, 'Suicide Patterns and Trends in People of Indian Sub-Continent and Caribbean Origin in England and Wales', *Ethnicity and Health*, 1 (1), 1996: 55–63.

6   D. Bhugra et al., *Attempted Suicide in West London; 1. Rates Across Ethnic Communities* and *Attempted Suicide in West London; ll. Inter-group Comparisons of Asian and White Groups*, 1999. See also review of some current research on Asian female suicide in M. I. Husain, W. Waheed and N. Husain, *Self-harm in British South Asian women: psychosocial correlates and strategies for prevention*, Annals of General Psychiatry, 22 May 2006, available at www.pubmedcentral.nih.gov/articlerender.fcgi?artid=1538599. Accessed 20/2/11.

7   Mayor of London, *The Way Forward: Taking action to end violence against women and girls. Final Strategy 2010–2013*, 2010.

8   See *Domestic Violence, Forced Marriage and 'Honour'-Based Violence: Sixth report of Session 2007–8, Vol I*, House of Commons, Home Affairs Select Committee, May 2008, pp. 5, 17.

9   See *Safe and Sane*.

10   R. K. Thiara and S. Roy, *Vital Statistics: The experiences of Black, Asian, Minority Ethnic and Refugee women and children facing violence and abuse*, Imkaan, 2010.

11   See case of 'Rani' in *Safe and Sane*, p. 78.

12   See Brittain et al. in *Black and Minority Ethnic Women in the UK*. London: The Fawcett Society, 2005

13   In the 1970s, SBS campaigned with other groups to ban virginity testing at Heathrow airport by immigration officials on south Asian brides. The officials assumed that Asian women would be virgins if they were genuine fiancées entering the UK to join their British would-be husbands.

14   Hansard, *Adjournment Debate on Human Rights (Women)*. London: House of Commons, 325, 8–16 February 1999.

15   NHS London Strategic Health Authority, *Independent investigation into the care and treatment provided to Mrs S by the West London Mental Health trust and Ealing Primary Care Trust*, NHS, London, 2010.

16　Surjit Athwal was murdered in a so-called 'honour killing' by her husband and mother-in-law in 1998 while on a trip to India because she wanted a divorce. The suspects were not convicted until 2007 and her body has never been found.

17　*R v Harcharan Dhaliwal*, 7 March 2006, Central Criminal Court.

18　*Quila and Aquilar, and Bibi and Mohammed v Secretary of State for the Home Department*, Court of Appeal, 12 December 2010.

19　*Kaur and Shah v London Borough of Ealing*, 2008.

20　See M. Coy, L. Kelly and J. Foord, *Map of Gaps 2*, End Violence against Women coalition and the Equalities and Human Rights Commission, 2009.

21　See David Cameron's speech at the Munich Security Conference, on 5 February 2011, at http://www.number10.gov.uk/news/speeches-and-transcripts/2011/02/pms-speech-at-munich-security-conference-60293. Accessed 20/2/11.

22　See Muslim Arbitration Panel, *Report – Liberation from Forced Marriage*, London, Muslim Arbitration Panel, 2008. See also http://www.matribunal.com/arbact.html. Accessed 20/2/11.

Conclusion

The stories and reflections all link together; that's the whole point of this book. The experiences of marriage, divorce, cross-cultural relationships, circumcision, domestic violence all weave together in ways that I would never have expected.

This passage is taken from Isha's reflections on this volume in which she neatly highlights why the stories and experiences recounted have been placed side by side. The narratives shared with readers thread together, and although each chapter reveals distinct experiences because of the differences that tradition and culture produce, common strands can be pulled out. The commonality running throughout is the underlying cause of the storytellers' discomfort which is not solely or even primarily concerned with culture, religion or tradition, but rather is down to a combination of two dimensions: firstly, the racial and class-based infrastructure shaping the secular society they inhabit; and secondly, the patriarchal gendered ideology that to differing extents and levels shapes the world-view of both diaspora groups and the state. Each of the stories reveals how women from different BME backgrounds endure various forms of exclusion. This exclusion is seen in a lack of engagement between secular state agencies and specific BME groups of women. The state remains largely ignorant of the individual cultural practices and the traditional beliefs that sustain them, which in turn limit the life opportunities of BME women. For example, in Chapter 6 we learnt that dowry is not legislated against in the UK even though in India it is held responsible for a large number of atrocities against women and has been illegal since 1961. In chapters 4 and 5, we learn that little significant research has been conducted on the levels of domestic violence in the Zimbabwean and Bangladeshi diaspora. In addition to this lack of base-line data on the levels of domestic violence, there is a lack of any understanding of how women respond to it given the lack of BME tailored state support services. In Chapter 2 Isha highlighted that no definitive research has been commissioned by government into the prevalence of FGM among the Somali community in the UK. This lack of knowledge about BME women's lives and commitment to monitor instances of gender-based violence is indicative of state agencies and officials that have not fully embraced gender and racial equality.

This lack of knowledge of BME women's lives is also due to confusion over how relevant data can be effectively and ethically gathered. If we take the case of FGM, this practice is heavily legislated against in the UK, and public and government awareness is reasonably high. There is also widespread agreement that this practice is brutal and unjust; these sentiments are widely communicated and those within the Somali community who believe FGM is necessary are therefore unlikely to share their views openly with those they feel oppose the practice. Furthermore, as one of Isha's storytellers reveals, a significant number of the fiercest supporters of FGM are in fact women who themselves have been circumcised. In the story retold in Chapter 2, a mother talked of wanting to ensure her daughter's 'honour' by arranging her circumcision. However, Ishaman also lived a traditional patriarchal life: she did not work and her husband monitored closely her movements, insisting that he was present for the interview. How easy is it for an outsider to access and discuss FGM with Somali women who rarely step outside of culturally sanctioned spaces such as the home, mosque or family gatherings? The answer is clearly, not easy at all, but this book also presents the solution. Outsiders cannot be used to collect this kind of insight; instead, researchers from inside diaspora communities – such as those involved in this book – should be encouraged to sensitively record women's experiences from within their communities. Their role is to make visible the array of responses women express about specific traditions. These responses will reveal something about the role tradition plays in affirming a woman's identity whilst also highlighting condemnation of practices that infringe on a person's freedom and rights. Making audible internal voices that challenge practices helps stronger activism to emerge. The cases recorded in this volume highlight the importance of opening up more spaces for women to engage in dialogue across the divide of opposing views. In other words women from within the same community who hold different attitudes about the importance of specific practices could be encouraged to explore together the views they hold and the reasons for them. These dialogues in many instances are already happening and although they are highly emotive and fragile, they are crucial to the feminist agenda of eradicating gender-based violence. Through and out of such communication views change as participants hear different experiences, reactions and perspectives.

In the Introduction and Chapter 1 the ethical pitfalls of this approach were discussed; in particular, the difficult position of the researchers or story-recipients was explored. It is challenging for those inside a community to switch their positioning and become researchers, observing and documenting the behaviour and views of those they would otherwise live alongside. It may, for some, feel as if they are informing on those they care about. However, the approach taken in this volume utilised aspects of the oral or life histories approach and has enabled researchers to sensitively draw out a woman's views and experiences articulated in her own words. As detailed in the first chapter, the life histories or oral histories approach is designed to destabilise the power relationship between researcher and researched. For much of this volume a more equal relationship was signified by the language used to describe this relationship. For example, the terms 'researcher' and 'researched' have been replaced by the terms 'storyteller' and 'story-recipient'. The storyteller is largely in control of this process, and although it may take a while for specific information to emerge, the pace and nature of what is revealed is determined by them. Although in many chapters the story-recipients found it difficult to urge their storytellers to focus on sharing their life narratives, and other qualitative techniques were employed, the starting point and intention throughout was to tease out experiences through storytelling. At points the storytellers themselves made the decision to shift from recounting their experiences chronologically to sharing their views and opinions on issues. We see this, for example, in Chapter 6 when the women Charlenie spent time with frankly shared their views about dowry and women's position more widely within *Brahmin* Hindu families. Although the flow of discussion may have shifted from a biographical narrative to an airing of views, the storytellers were nonetheless in control. The views shared reflected their priorities and in fact by documenting the conversation that unfolded Charlenie allowed readers to glimpse something of how the women view aspects of their lives.

I return now to a question posed and discussed in the Introduction to this volume which has been picked up in various ways throughout: why should religion, culture and tradition form part of the lens through which we think about the experiences of BME women? I believe this study has shown that using religion, culture and tradition as the starting point for discussion of the life experiences of different groups of women enables a number of close insights to emerge. By focusing on specific practices and asking women to talk about their experiences of them, each chapter has revealed something about how women creatively manage their situations and work through barriers preventing them from living the kind of lives they desire. The insights recorded highlight how women utilise rather than reject their cultural and religious heritage, treating them often as resources to understand negative experiences or to draw on positively in the quest to manipulate and create better situations. For example, in Chapter 3 Ebyan highlights how problems in marriage are often talked about and shared during another woman's marriage ceremony. Somali women carve out within their cultural and religious traditions spaces within which they share stories and work through the challenges they face. In Chapter 4 Esline also in both stories highlights how her storytellers drew on or tapped into church networks in order to gain the strength needed to take the courageous step and leave a life of violence. The church buildings and the networks around them offered both her storytellers a bolt hole. They turned to the church for companionship, as many run specific groups for women offering fellowship and opportunities for problem sharing.

Deborah Gaitskell (2002, 2004) has written about the role of women's church organisations in South Africa. In particular, she has studied the emergence of the Anglican Women's fellowship network in post-apartheid South Africa and explored how such organisations are becoming more prominent as platforms from which women can influence national and international political decision making. In her work on local church-based organisations across Christian denominations she found them to play an important function, offering support to women in their everyday lives. In the case of the Anglican Women's fellowship some have now grown outwards from local contexts and joined with others to form national and even transnational movements that actively campaign on issues that threaten people's stability and well-being. She highlights the close-knit bonds that emerge between women involved in these organisations. Although the research in this book did not focus on women's support networks, the stories and accounts shared in chapters 3 and 4 highlight the extent to which support networks often emerge out of religious spaces and institutions. I will return to the role such localised support networks play in the lives of BME women.

In Chapter 5 Noorjahan details how her informants ask for help within their immediate cultural and religious community, and whilst this support does not always urge women to leave vulnerable situations, acknowledgement was given to each woman that what they were enduring was not right. This in some way must have been self-affirming and provided much needed motivation to continue day-to-day life albeit under the continued veil of violence and/or fear of it. However, the advice given can lead to ambiguous conclusions, since the religious leadership do not view violence against women as a serious offence that requires immediate action. In the stories told in Chapter 5 each woman was able to find support and people to talk through her situation within her immediate diaspora community.

Although many of the chapters highlight how women find support within their communities, either from other women, family or from prominent local figures, most chapters also reveal how aspects of culture and religion let women down. As has already been touched on, religious leaders in chapters 2 and 5 do not stand up and publically condemn the violence and brutality of FGM. In Chapter 4 the imams do not challenge the way in which domestic violence is normalised in women's lives. In highlighting these failings the chapters also provide evidence that the current government drive towards raising the profile of religious leadership – because it is assumed they have influence over local communities – is naïve and will do little to end the injustices BME women face. Again, I will return to this argument later.

The motivations behind the decisions women make came through clearly. For example, the motivation for women to choose to conform to a cultural tradition seems to be twofold. Firstly, women conform because there are very few options, as the story in Chapter 3 highlights. Secondly, women opt to maintain the status quo because it offers them something they believe to be important, namely stability, security and a sense of rootedness. Conforming to tradition offers women grounding and a sense of identity despite the diversity of the secular society they live in. This security of knowing who you are is particularly important when the state you inhabit is hostile towards your difference and unable to respond to your experiences (see chapters 5 and 7). The stories, in revealing the decision-making processes of at least some BME women, expose a stark lack of real choice. In Esline's chapter it took Mary a long time to step outside her door and seek out support. No one came to her; she had to undergo a conscious change alone in which she acknowledged the abuse she was suffering and took the decision to act. Had she received support earlier or felt safe enough in the environment outside her door, she may well have been able to take the steps to leave her husband much sooner. As already stated, she turned first not to secular agencies but to her local church.

Religion and culture make important contributions as analytical constructs included in a continuum to help us understand why gender-based violence persists. Religion, however, is part of the problem, not just because its leadership is usually male and promotes ideas about the world that favour the interests of a male elite, but also because religion, as detailed in chapters 2 and 7, provides the authority needed to justify cultural practices such as dowry and FGM. In other words, religious teachings endorse the values and beliefs founding traditional practices. Religion as part of the problem will not be solved by ignoring it – isolating it from discussion about gender-based violence is not the answer. In fact Benthall (2008) argues persuasively that religion has always been there and is unlikely to ever disappear as a formidable structural force in both secular and non-secular societies. He offers explanation drawing on the work of Bourdieu (1977) who, like Weber, argued that society cannot be analysed simply in terms of economic classes and ideologies. He developed the terms of *doxa* and *habitus* to denote a relationship between a subconscious and structured field of human experiences. Within the *doxa*, subconscious beliefs and concepts exist that through the *habitus* form ideas about how individuals should live and behave in the world. Religion plays a significant role in perpetuating symbols that rest in the subconscious but then later find expression in an array of articulated beliefs, practices and institutions. Religions possess a great capacity to evolve and adapt to an ever-changing world, perhaps because deep-rooted subconscious symbols, feelings and impulses support the belief systems on which they are based. It is impossible to prove why religion is so permanent, and certainly there will be various explanations. The institutional structures of religious traditions, the emphasis on divine knowledge, and the hierarchal relationships upon which most are based, hold something of a clue. Adherents look to their leadership for guidance and in turn religious leaders are thought to have gained their wisdom from a higher being.

The volume in different places has looked at the level of support women may receive from religious leaders at times of trauma such as marital breakdown and/or domestic violence. As already stated, male authority perpetuated through the institutional structures of religion does little to challenge underlying patterns of gender inequality and reinforces women's dependence on men, rendering them vulnerable to abuse and oppression. The patriarchal foundations of religious traditions form the basis for cultural values and beliefs which become embedded in people's world-view through practices such as FGM and dowry. A chain exists through which patriarchal values are engrained at every level. Religious structures including institutions and leadership help maintain this chain by conveying authoritative ideas about how people should live. The gendered ideology generated and communicated by religion is then transplanted into everyday life through cultural practices. What the stories in this volume have shown is that, whilst the end point may differ, with many different cultural practices existing, the starting point is the same. The foundations of gender-based violence are without doubt patriarchal but this ideology would not be able to take hold without the authority religion provides. Religion rests on a male construct of the divine as the ultimate source of wisdom and truth beyond reproach and is therefore a definitive source of authority used to perpetuate gender ideals that are inherently patriarchal even in a secular state (King, 1995).

As discussed in Bradley (2010, a and b) I also believe that the experiential dimension to religion helps to sustain its importance in people's lives. Many religious spaces are intensely private but also safe. For example, in the context of Christianity and Islam it is difficult for anyone to invade the internal reflective moment created through individual prayer. Similarly in Hinduism many women-only rituals are practised that serve a similar purpose, ensuring that the individual has at least these moments to deeply reflect on their lives. In situations where no other support or opportunities for personal reflection exist, religion becomes crucial, providing a practical function in women's lives, a chance to take time out from the demands of daily life and take stock, address and acknowledge problems and work through responses.

The stories documented here did not touch on the role that an individual's personal faith or spirituality has in shaping how they might respond to the patriarchal foundations of their tradition and the implications it may have for them. Also, the volume did not explore how the spiritual dimension to religion helps individuals express personhood and enact their role in life. However, ethnographic work exists that focuses on this aspect of religion and highlights that personal experiences of religion are hugely important, providing moments for critical reflection out of which individuals may take decisions to challenge practices or situations that are harming them (see Bradley, 2010 a, 2010 b). However, as already alluded to, the harm religion brings to women's lives must remain one of the central foci in campaigns to end gender-based violence. Worryingly, secular government policy in the UK, rather than condemning and questioning the influence religious leaders have in contributing to women's vulnerability, is working and consulting more closely with them.

Problems with the secular state

Labour government policy embraced a concept of 'community cohesion', which to some extent continues to influence the approach taken today. Policy formulated around community cohesion has tended to explore ways of promoting a liberal, secular value base across Britain's diverse communities. In turn this policy has practically involved the identification of key local figures with whom, it is assumed, other community members consult. These figures are thought to wield a degree of influence which if captured by secular state agencies could be used to promote government policy. In many instances, and as Hannana Siddiqui discussed in her chapter, officials have mistakenly assumed that these 'influential figures' are in tune with the diverse experiences and needs of their community and indeed have the well-being of all in mind. Religious leaders have emerged as key figures in government campaigns to bring diaspora groups more squarely into the fold so that their activities can be closely monitored and if necessary curbed. The motivation behind the push to engage more effectively with local communities, especially ethnic minority groups, is obviously linked with post-9/11 government concerns to actively eradicate extremist and terrorist tendencies. Money has been channelled into a range of projects including training programmes that target religious leaders, urging them to disseminate pro-government and anti-radical messages. These initiatives form part of the 'prevent strategy', launched in 2007 to stop people becoming terrorists or supporting terrorism both in the UK and overseas. They are, in other words, part of the preventative strand of the government's counter-terrorism strategy, 'contest'. According to Oxfam (2009), the unintended effects of *Prevent* fall into three areas: 'The first is the impact of cuts in funding to organisations working in poor ethnic minority communities, as part of a shift away from "single group" funding and towards community cohesion. The second is the discrimination experienced by ethnic minority communities because of the targeting of Muslims by *Prevent*. The third is the way in which ethnic minority women may become more vulnerable because *Prevent* and cohesion policy puts more power and authority into the hands of religious leaders and interfaith networks.'

In the first area, Oxfam is concerned about the impact of cutting funding to race-equality organisations, such as those supporting Pakistanis and Bangladeshis, as part of the move to community cohesion and *Prevent* policy. In a series of interviews in Oldham, *Peacemaker* revealed that funding was diverted to mainstream organisations who did not pick up the support needs of those communities when the race equality organisations closed, leaving people from deprived communities worse off, heightening their poverty and exclusion. Oxfam are particularly concerned about the effects of the *Prevent* agenda on BME women:

> Our partner *Southall Black Sisters* researched the impact of community cohesion policy on their beneficiaries experiencing domestic violence. The way in which the *Prevent* and community cohesion agenda funds religious organisations, accompanied by cuts in funding to specialist women's organisations, increase the vulnerability of BME women. Interviews conducted *by Southall Black Sisters* report how women feel caught between the demands of religion and family. They need advice from professionals to secure their own safety and rights to protection as women under British law, and the role of specialist women's organisations in getting them out of danger is critical. In Oxfam's view the risks for vulnerable women in cutting funding is an unacceptable result of cohesion and *Prevent* policy, and warrants further research and examination. (Oxfam, 2009)

The stories in this volume offer further evidence that more, not less, specialised support is needed as BME women struggle with multiple layers of prejudice, marginalisation and in many cases abuse. Additional concerns over the level of BME women's marginalisation arise as a result of the current government's removal of multiculturalism as the underlying value base of society and its replacement with the ambiguous term 'Big Society'. The current concept of the 'Big Society', as with *Prevent*, aims to see minority groups embrace more wholeheartedly a sense of belonging to one 'British' society. As the stories in this book attest, secular British society has not reached out to BME women. Religious leaders are generally not prioritising the needs of women and remain unwilling to acknowledge the extent to which gender-based violence exists in their communities. This emphasis on all groups uniting under a patriotic banner of Britishness makes it even harder to appreciate and respond to the variety of different experiences women have of living in the UK. This distancing from 'difference' will make it even less likely that the specific needs of BME women will be acknowledged and met by the state.

So what is meant by this term 'Big Society'? The government indicated that it refers to 'communities feeling empowered to solve problems in their neighbourhood, having the freedom to influence and discuss topics that matter to them, and a more local approach to social action and responsibility'. David Cameron says he wants this government to 'be the first in a generation to leave office with much less power than it started with'. He goes on, 'What this is all about is giving people more power and control to improve their lives and communities' (BBC, 2011). On first hearing this notion of a 'Big Society' and the accompanying definition, there is little to raise concern. The concepts of 'empowerment' and 'freedom' seem to be entrenched at the heart of this vision. However, it is the practical realities that lie behind it that alarm those active in working with BME women. 'Big Society' for many is government code for efficiency, which in turn signals a reduction in funding. This, coupled with the maintenance of the *Prevent* strategy, means that money is unlikely to be removed from initiatives designed to curb the threat of terrorism, but instead local community-based, specialist organisations such as Southall Black Sisters will see their funding cut yet again. The types of gender-based violence echoing throughout this volume, the personal struggles women face growing up in a BME community within a secular state, will only intensify. A 'Big Society' leaves no space to celebrate difference or acknowledge the ways in which women are marginalised and subjected to abuse. Responsibility for responding to abuse is being driven down further to the community level without any resources to help activists challenge structural, gender-based inequalities. This volume in some ways represents a political space that the authors have used to give voice to struggles as well as to convey positive self-images. I hope it can make something of a contribution towards highlighting the urgent need for gender to take centre stage in the formation of government policy. The refusal of governments to mainstream a gender approach in both their dialogue with different communities and in the strategies they evolve is reflective of their own patriarchal underpinnings, and here lies the impenetrable problem. BME women are reliant on a secular state that itself co-opts and perpetuates patriarchy in similar ways to their own cultures, religions and traditions. It is therefore no surprise that FGM, dowry and domestic violence flourish within secular states.

This discussion leads me to the question I asked some of my contributors: what difference does migration make to BME women? One replied, and the others agreed, that 'in many ways things become worse, women become more isolated, find it even harder to talk about the things they would like to change in their lives. Practices such as FGM and domestic violence continue here. Many Somali parents continue to take their children abroad to be circumcised and if they can't afford this they get it done here.'

At the start of this book, in both the Introduction and in Chapter 1, I tackled the ethical difficulties with any research that seeks to get close insights into the lives of others. The discomfort some of the researchers experienced highlighted the ethical problems with this kind of research. Many of the stories told here could so easily be used by others as proof that the cultures and traditions from which the women in this volume come are problematic and must be challenged and, at the extreme, eradicated. The blame therefore shifs from the state, which should possess the capacity to reach out to and understand women's experiences, to the individual minority groups who are told their traditions are not in line with the secular 'Big Society'. Behind the discourse of the 'Big Society' is the belief that communities should take responsibility for sorting out their own inequalities. Religious leaders are empowered to assert their influence even more strongly at a community level. This approach condemns BME women to an even more marginal existence; their needs will be further buried by the secular state.

This volume intended to highlight the overlapping themes emerging throughout that pinpoint patriarchy as the cause of women's problems. However, the stories told here have shown that culture, religion and secularism play a part in perpetuating and transmitting gendered messages, embedding and normalising male superiority. These values are embedded in the state which means many women experience patriarchal oppression twice, both internal to their immediate families and community and then in the wider society. This perhaps explains why the women whose stories are told here have struggled to carve out the kinds of lives they dream of. Until the wider societal and underlying structures are changed to endorse the principle of gender equality, women from all backgrounds will continue to struggle to be heard. This bleak concluding statement must be balanced against the positive narratives of women celebrating their identities and working together to shape meaningful and contented lives. Despite the struggles, the women whose stories are recorded here would not change who they are, as Ebyan clearly declared, 'I am proud to be a Somali woman.' Readers should distinguish between the structures of the state, and aspects of culture and tradition that limit women's potential to live freely and women's own sense of self which more often than not is defiant, optimistic and wholly positive.

References

Abu-Lughod, L., 'Do Muslim women really need saving? Anthropological reflections on cultural relativism and its others', *American Anthropology*, 104 (3), 2002: 783–90.

Ahmed, D. S., *Gendering the Spirit: Women, Religion and the Post Colonial Response*, London: Zed Press, 2002.

Alexander, U., *Only the Eyes are Mine*, New Delhi: Frog Books, 2005.

Al-Shaykh, H., *The Locust and the Bird: My Mothers' Story*, London: Bloomsbury, 2009.

Armstrong, A., *Culture and Choice: Lessons from Survivors of Gender Violence in Zimbabwe*, Harare: Violence Against Women in Zimbabwe Research Project, 1998.

Asad, T., *Genealogies of Religion: Discipline and Reasons of Power in Christianity and Islam*, Baltimore: John Hopkins University Press, 1992.

Benthall, J., *Returning to Religion: Why a Secular Aga is Haunted by Faith*, London and New York: I.B.Tauris, 2008.

Berns McGown, R., *Muslims in the Diaspora: The Somali Community of London and Toronto*, Toronto: University of Toronto Press, 1999.

Beyer, P., *Religion and Globalization*, London: Sage, 1994.

Beyer, P. and Beaman, C. (eds), *Religion, Globalization and Culture*. Oxford: Brill, 2007.

Bloch, A., *The Development Potential of Zimbabweans in the Diaspora: A Survey of Zimbabweans in the UK and South Africa*, Geneva: International Organisation for Migration, 2005.

— 'Zimbabweans in Britain: Transnational Activities and Capabilities', *Journal of Ethnic and Migration Studies*, 34, 2, 2008: 287–305.

Bourdieu, P., *Outline of Theory and Practice*, Cambridge: Cambridge University Press, 1977.

Bowie, F., *The Anthropology of Religion: An Introduction*, Oxford: Blackwell, 2000.

Bradley, T., *Challenging the NGOs: Women and Western Discourses in India*. London and New York: I.B.Tauris, 2006.

— 'Physical religious spaces in the lives of Rajasthani village women: the ethnographic study and practice of religion in development', *Journal of Human Development*, 10, 1, 2009: 43–62.

— a. *Gender and Religion in the Developing World: Faith-Based Organisations and Feminism in India*, London: I.B.Tauris, 2010.

Bradley, T. and Tomalin, E. (eds), *Dowry: Bridging the Gap between Theory and Practice*, New Delhi and London: Women Unlimited and Zed Books, 2009.

Cameron, David, 'Big Society is my mission', BBC News, 14 February 2011, http://www.bbc.co.uk/news/uk-politics-12443396.

Crenshaw, K., 'Mapping the margins: intersectionality, identity, politics and violence against women of color', Stanford Law Review, 43 (6), 1993: 1241–58.

Dirie, L. G., 'A hospital study of the complications of female circumcision', *Tropical Doctor*, 21 (4), Oct. 1991: 146–8.

Divie, M., 'Female circumcision in Somalia and women's motives', *Acta Obstetricia et Gynecologica Scandinavia*, 70 (7–8), 1991: 581–85.

— 'The risk of medical complications after female circumcision', *East African Medical Journal*, 2 (2), 1992: 195, 214.

Dorkenoo, E. L., Morison, L. and Macfarlane, A., *A Statistical Study to Estimate the Prevalence of Female Genital Mutilation in England and Wales*, Foundation for Women's Health, Research and Development (FORWARD) in collaboration with the London School of Hygiene and Tropical Medicine and the Department of Midwifery, City University, Department of Health, England, 2007.

Gaitskell, D., 'Whose heartland and which periphery? Christian women crossing South Africa's racial divide in the twentieth century', *Women History Review*, 11, 3, 2002: 375–95.

— 'Crossing boundaries and building bridges: the Anglican Women's Fellowship in post apartheid South Africa', *Journal of Religion in Africa*, 34, 3, 2004.

Gruenbaum, E., *The Female Circumcision Controversy: An Anthropological Perspective*, Philadelphia: University of Philadelphia Press, 2001.

Guerin, P., Hussein, E. and Guerin, B., 'Weddings and parties: cultral healing in one community of Somali women', *Austrialian e-journal for the advancement of mental health*, 5 (2), 2006.

Harding, J. and Gabriel, J., 'Communities in the making: pedagogic explorations using oral history', *International Studies in the Sociology of Education*, 14, 3, 2004: 185–201

Horowitz, C. R., 'Female circumcision: African women confront American medicine', *Journal of General Internal Medicine*, 331, 1997: 712–16.

Karaya, D., *Female Genital Mutilation in Africa*, Longwood, USA: Xulon, 2003.

Kelly, L., 'Inside outsiders: mainstreaming violence against women into human rights discourse and practice', *International Feminist Journal of Politics*, 7 (4), 2005: 471–95.

King, U., *Religion and Gender*, Oxford: Wiley Blackwell, 1994.

— 'Religion and Gender', in L. Jones (ed.), *Macmillan Encyclopedia of Religion*, New York: Macmillan Reference Books, 2005.

King, U. and Beattie, T. (eds), *Gender, Religion and Diversity: Cross Cultural Perspectives*, London and New York: Continuum, 2004.

Kishwar, M. (a), 'Who am I? Living identities Vs Acquired ones', *Manushi*, May–June, 1996.

— (b), 'Yes to Sita, No to Ram! The continuing popularity of Sita in India', *Manushi*, Jan.–Feb., 1996.

— 'Laws against domestic violence: underused or abused?', *Manushi*, Sept.–Oct. (120), 2000.

Leslie, J., *The Perfect Wife (Stridharmapaddhati)*, Delhi: Oxford University Press, 1989.

Lochat, H., *Female Genital Mutilation: Treating the Tears*, London: Middlesex University Press, 2004.

Mai, M., *In the Name of Honour*, London: Virago Press, 2007.

Mernissi, F., *The Veil and the Male Elite: A Feminist Interpretation of Women's Rights in Islam*, Berkeley: Persus Books, 1992.

McGregor, J., '"Joining the BBC (British Bottom Cleaners)": Zimbabwean migrants and the UK care industry', *Journal of Ethnic and Migration Studies*, 33, 5, 2007: 801–24.

— 'Abject spaces, transnational calculations: Zimbabweans in Britain navigating work, class and the law', *Transactions of the Institute of British Geographers*, 33, 4, 2008: 466–82.

— 'Associational links with home among Zimbabweans in the UK: reflections on long-distance nationalisms', *Global Networks*, 9, 2, 2009: 185–208.

McGregor, J. and Primorac, R. (eds), *Zimbabwe's New Diaspora: Displacement and the Cultural Politics of Survival*, Oxford: Berghahn Books, 2010.

Miller, K.. 'Female circumcision: challenges to the practice as a human rights violation', *Harvard Journal of Law and Gender*, 2, 3, 1985: 113–26.

Mohanty, C., 'Under Western Eyes' in Mohanty, C. and Russo, A. (eds), *Third World Women and the Politics of Feminism*, Bloomington: Indiana University Press, 1988.

Morison, L. A., Dirir, A., Elmi, Sada, Warsame, J. and Dirir, S., 'How experiences and attitudes relating to female circumcision vary according to age on arrival in Britain: a study among young Somalis in London', *Ethnicity & Health*, 9 (1), 2004: 75–100

Momoh, C. (ed.), *Female Genital Mutilation*, Oxford: Radcliffe Publishing, 2005.

Narayan, U., *Dislocating Cultures: Identities, Tradition and Third World Feminism*, New York: Routledge, 1997.

Nnaemeka, O., *Female Circumcision and the Politics of Knowledge: African Women in Imperial Discourses*, New York: Praeger, 2005.

Nyangweso Wangila, M., *Female Circumcision: The Interplay of Religion, Culture and Gender in Kenya*, New York: Orbis Books, 2007.

Ofei-Aboagye, R., 'Domestic violence in Ghana', *Signs*, 19, 4, 1994: 924–38.

Oxfam. 2009. 'Oxfam submission to Department for Communities and Local Government, new inquiry and call for evidence issued in the session 2008–09', Memorandum from Oxfam (PVE 12), 21 July 2009, http://www.publications.parliament.uk/pa/cm200910/cmselect/cmcomloc/65/65we11.htm.

Pasura, D., *Mapping Exercise: Zimbabwe*, 2006. Available at: http://www.iomlondon.org/doc/mapping/Zimbabwe%20Mapping%20Exercise%20Final%20Report.pdf.

— 'Gendering the diaspora: Zimbabwean migrants in Britain', *African Diaspora*, 1 (1–2), 2008: 86–109.

Patel, P. and Siddiqui, H., 'Shrinking Secular Spaces: Asian Women at the Intersect of Race, Religion and Gender', in *Violence Against Women in South Asian Communities: Issues for Policy and Practice*, London: Jessica Kingsley Publishers, 2010.

Ramage, A. S., Strauss, L. and McEwen, A., 'Somali women's experience of childbirth in the UK: perspectives from Somali health workers', *Midwifery*, 25 (2), 2009: 181–86.

Reychler, L. and Paffenholz, T., *Peace Building: A Field Guide*, Boulder, CO: Lynne Reinner, 2000.

Rogo, K. et al., 'Female genital cutting, women's health and development: the role of the World Bank,' *African Human Development Series*, Working Paper 122, 2007.

Schneider, E., *Battered Women and Feminist Law Making*, New Haven, CT: Yale University Press, 2000.

Sen, P. and Kelly, L., *Violence Against Women in the UK: A CEDAW Thematic Report*, 2009.

Shell-Duncan, B. and Hernlund, Y., *Female Circumcision in African Culture: Controversy and Change*, Boulder, CO: Lynne Reinner Publishers, 2007.

Sokoloff, N. J. and Dupont, I., 'Domestic violence at the intersections of race, class and gender: challenges and contributions to understanding violence against marginalized women in diverse communities', *Violence Against Women* 11 (1), 2005: 38–64.

Stewart, S., 'Working the System: Sensitizing the Police to the Plight of Women in Zimbabwe', in M. Schuler, *Freedom from Violence: Strategies from Around the World*, New York: UNIFEM, 1992: pp. 157–71.

Teltumbde, A., *The Persistence of Caste: The Khairlanji Murders and India's Hidden Apartheid*, London: Zed Books, 2010.

Thiara, R. K. and Gill, A. K. (eds), *Violence Against Women in South Asian Communities: Issues for Policy and Practice*, London: Jessica Kingsley Publishers, 2010.

Toubia, N., 'Female circumcision and public health', *New England Journal of Medicine*, 331, 1994: 712–16.

Van Der Kwaak, A., 'Female circumcision and gender identity: a question of alliance?', *Social Science and Medicine*, 35 (6), 1992: 777–87.

West, R., 'The difference in women's hedonic lives: a phenomenological critique of feminist legal theory', *Wisconsin Women's Law Journal*, 3, 1987: 81–145.

Wilson, A., *Dreams, Questions, Struggles: South Asian Women in Britain*, London: Pluto Press, 2006.

Wing, A. K. and Smith, M. N., 'Critical race feminism lifts the veil: Muslim women, France and the headscarf ban', *UC Davis Law Review*, 39 (3), 2006: 743–90

Index

About Zed Books

Zed Books is a critical and dynamic publisher, committed to increasing awareness of important international issues and to promoting diversity, alternative voices and progressive social change. We publish on politics, development, gender, the environment and economics for a global audience of students, academics, activist and general readers. Run as a co-operative, we aim to operate in an ethical and environmentally sustainable way.

Find out more at:

www.zedbooks.co.uk

For up-to-date news, articles, reviews and events information visit:

http://zed-books.blogspot.com

We can also be found on **Facebook**, **ZNet**, **Twitter** and **Library Thing**.